W9-BGK-645

INTRODUCING EGYPTIAN HIEROGLYPHS

INTRODUCING
EGYPTIAN HIEROGLYPHS

BY

BARBARA WATTERSON

SCOTTISH ACADEMIC PRESS
EDINBURGH

Published by
Scottish Academic Press Ltd.
33 Montgomery Street, Edinburgh EH7 5JX

ISBN 0 7073 0267 6

© 1981 Scottish Academic Press Ltd

All rights reserved. No part of this publication may be reproduced, stored in a retrieval system, or transmitted, in any form, or by any means, electronic, mechanical, photocopying, recording or otherwise, without the prior permission of the Scottish Academic Press Ltd., 33 Montgomery Street, Edinburgh EH7 5JX.

Reprinted 1982, 1983

Printed in Great Britain by
Clark Constable (1982) Ltd., Edinburgh

CONTENTS

Contents

Contents

ABBREVIATIONS

adj.	adjective
adv.	adverb
cf.	*confer* = compare
dep. pron.	dependent pronoun
det.	determinative(s)
e.g.	*exempli gratia* = for instance
f.	feminine
ideo.	ideogram
lit.	literally
m.	masculine
phon.	phonetically
prep.	preposition
sing.	singular
var., varr.	variant(s)

PART I

**General introduction and background
to hieroglyphic writing in Egypt
and to the principles of picture writing**

OUTLINE OF EGYPTIAN CHRONOLOGY

Dates B.C. (approx.)	Periods	Dynasties	Principal kings
c. 7000-5000	Palaeolithic	—	—
c. 5000-3100	Neolithic	Predynastic cultures Upper Egypt: Badarian Naqada I & II Lower Egypt: Fayum Merimde	—
c. 3100-2890	Archaic	I	Menes/Narmer
c. 2890-2686		II	
c. 2686-2613		III	Zoser
c. 2613-2494	Old Kingdom	IV	Sneferu, Cheops, Chephren, Mycerinus
c. 2494-2345		V	Sahure, Niuserre, Unas
c. 2345-2181		VI	Teti, Pepi
c. 2181-2160	First	VII, VIII	Memphite kings
c. 2160-2040	Intermediate	IX, X	Herakleopolitan kings
2134-1991	Middle	XI	Theban kings
1991-1786	Kingdom	XII	(from 2040 ruled over whole of Egypt)

Dates B.C. (approx.)	Periods	Dynasties	Principal kings
1786-1551	Second Intermediate	XIII, XIV XV, XVI, XVII	Hyksos kings
1551-1310	New Kingdom	XVIII	Amenophis, Tuthmosis, Hatshepsut, Akhenaten, Tutankhamun
1310-1198		XIX	Seti, Ramesses II
1198-1087		XX	Ramesses III-XI
1087-945	Third Intermediate	XXI	Psussenes in Tanis Priest-kings in Thebes
945-715		XXII	Sheshonq in Bubastis
819-720		XXIII	Libyan kings in Tanis
728-715		XXIV	Saite kings
716-664	Late Period	XXV	Ethiopian kings (Taharqa)
664-525		XXVI	Saite kings (Psammeticus)
525-404		XXVII	Persian domination (Cambyses, Darius, Xerxes)
404-378		XXVIII, XXIX	Last native kings
378-341		XXX	
341-332		XXXI	Persian domination (Darius III)

Dates B.C. to A.D.	Periods	Dynasties	Ruling Bodies & Kings
332-30	Ptolemaic	XXXII	Alexander the Great, Ptolemy, Cleopatra
30 B.C.-A.D. 284	Roman	—	
284-640	Byzantine	—	(*Christian Egypt*)
640	*Arab conquest*		(*Muslim Egypt*)
868		Tulunid	Ibn Tulun
969		Fatimid	
1171	Syrian	Ayyubid	Saladin
1250-1517	Turkish	Mameluke	
1516-1798	Ottoman		Pashas appointed by Turkish Sultan
1798			Napoleon
1801-1882	Turkish		Mehemet Ali (1801-1848)
1882-1919	British protectorate		
1919-1952	Independent but bound to Britain by Treaty		Farouk (1935-1952)
1952-present	Independent Republic		Gamel Abdel Nasser, Anwar Sadat, presidents

INTRODUCTION

In prehistoric times, possibly from about 6000 B.C., the population of Egypt was divided into tribal groups. Gradually, the tribes living in settlements on the banks of the Nile in the north of the country and the Delta came together to form the 'kingdom' of Lower Egypt; whilst the tribes who lived in the south of Egypt united to form the 'kingdom' of Upper Egypt.

Shortly before 3100 B.C. two important events took place. First, a new group of people, the so-called Armenoid or Giza race, entered Egypt via the Delta. It is not known where these people originated, but their skeletal remains show them to have been big-boned, big-skulled, more powerful than the indigenous tribes. They brought new talents and ideas with them; most importantly, they brought the idea of writing, and thus introduced Egypt into the historic era. The second important event was the conquest of Lower Egypt by an Upper Egyptian king named Narmer, who thus united the two halves of Egypt (known to the Egyptians as the Two Lands) under one ruler, himself.

The 3,000 years of Egyptian history which followed the unification of Egypt by King Narmer were divided into thirty dynasties of kings (roughly families of kings rather like our Tudor and Stuart dynasties) by the scholar-priest, Manetho, who lived in the third-century B.C., probably in the temple of Sebennytos in the Nile Delta. A chronology of Egypt, based on Manetho's system, is given on pages 3-5.

The most notable feature of the civilisation of Ancient Egypt was its buildings. Not houses, or even palaces, but temples and tombs. All Egyptians, from the king down to the poorest peasant, lived in houses built largely of mud-brick, wattle and daub—all perishable materials. Their gods, and their dead, were housed in monuments made of stone, designed, the Egyptians thought, to endure for eternity.

The passage of time, however, saw the disappearance of many Egyptian monumental buildings together with their contents. The Egyptians buried valuable grave goods with their dead. Human nature being what it is, the practice of tomb robbery is almost as old as the tombs themselves. The kings of Egypt were eager to build temples for their gods and tombs for themselves. They often found it expedient to use the material from a predecessor's buildings instead of quarrying for their own. Thus the depredations of men inflicted even more damage than those of Nature.

Of course, Ancient Egypt was ancient even to the Ancient Egyptians. A man born in Dynasty XX, around 1100 B.C., would have thought the Great Pyramid at Giza, one of the Seven Wonders of the Ancient World, built in Dynasty IV, very ancient—1,550 years old. The Great Pyramid was almost as remote in time from him as the Roman invasion of Britain in 55 B.C. is from us. If we consider that King Arthur, one of the legendary heroes of Britain, was probably a chieftain in late-Roman Britain who, if he existed at all, lived 1,550 years ago, we should not be surprised if the Egyptian of Dynasty XX knew as little of conditions in Egypt during Dynasty IV as we know of King Arthur and his times.

And so, throughout Egyptian history, time and human nature took their toll of Egypt's monuments. From around 500 B.C., Egypt suffered from foreign invaders who, in their turn, inflicted yet more damage. Assyrians, Persians, Greeks, Romans, all contributed to the disappearance of Ancient Egypt. The Romans, especially, were collectors of everything Egyptian. Great numbers of antiquities, from statues, large and small, to obelisks, those giant shafts of stone which can be many hundreds of tons in weight, were shipped back to Rome.

When Christianity came to Egypt, the destruction went on. The Egyptians abandoned the old temples and allowed sand to creep in. Eventually, they moved into the temples and used them as churches. Temples, and even tombs, were used as dwelling places. Where tomb and temple reliefs were not damaged deliberately because of religious fervour, or because of superstition and fear of the 'evil eye', they were damaged by dirt and misuse, and blackened by cooking fires.

Christian Egyptians were followed in the seventh-century A.D. by Moslems with the same attitudes towards their ancient pagan monuments. Even today, the fellahin of Egypt know that the soil from archaeological sites makes good sebakh, or fertiliser, and take whatever opportunities they can to obtain some.

The perennial enemy of all buildings in Egypt, ancient and modern, is sand. A constant battle has always had to be fought to keep them clear of it. Once Egypt had ceased to exist as a great civilisation (in 30 B.C. when, with the defeat of Antony and Cleopatra, she became a province of Rome) the battle to keep out the sand from her monuments was abandoned.

Much of what remained of Egypt's ancient monuments was lost beneath the sand for centuries. The sand, aided by Egypt's warm, dry climate, kept what was beneath it in a good state of preservation; and hid it from sight, thus saving it from destruction at the hands of men who were ignorant of what they were doing. Until, in the nineteenth-century A.D., men arrived in Egypt who were interested enough in her past to want to clear away the sand, to study what it had covered and preserved for centuries, and to value what they found.

Chapter I

NAPOLEON'S EXPEDITION TO EGYPT IN 1797

On 16th August 1797, Napoleon Bonaparte wrote : 'In order to destroy England utterly, we must get possession of Egypt.' Less than a year later, as the newly-appointed 'Commander of the army against England', he put his plan into action. He told his secretary, Bourrienne, that an invasion of England would be 'too chancy'. Instead, he proposed to invade Egypt. On 5th March 1798, the Directors of the French Republic empowered Napoleon to raise the army and fleet necessary to mount an expedition to Egypt.

Egypt had been a province of the Ottoman Empire since 1517 and was governed by a ruling class, the Mamelukes, who were descendants of Caucasian slave-troops originally brought to Egypt by the Turks in 1250. The first aim of Napoleon's Expedition to Egypt was to free the country from Turks and Mamelukes and bring it under the aegis of France. A secondary objective was to secure Egypt as a base from which to launch an attack on England's prize possession, India.

The third, and from an Egyptological point of view the most important, aim was an entirely original one for which Napoleon himself must be given credit. He would go to Egypt not only to 'improve the lot of the natives of Egypt' but, by instituting a programme of mapping, exploration, observation and recording, he would open up a country which was almost unknown to Europeans.

Thus, in the interests of scientific discovery, Napoleon began to recruit an army of artists, scientists and scholars. In less than three months, he had recruited 150 'learned civilians', amongst whom were Geoffroy Saint-Hilaire, naturalist ; Gratet de Dolomien, a mineralogist who gave his name to the Dolomites ; Dominique-Vivant Denon, draughtsman and engraver ; Claude Bertholet, chemist ; Dominique Larrey, surgeon ;

B

Guillaume Villoteau, musician; Marie-Jules de Savigny, botanist; Pierre Redouté, flower painter; and Nicolas Conté, the inventor of the lead pencil.

On 19th May 1798, Napoleon sailed from Toulon with 17,000 troops on board an armada of 180 ships. This fleet was supplemented by more than 200 ships sailing from Italian ports, enabling Napoleon to arrive in Egypt with an army of 55,000 men. They arrived at Marabout beach on the north coast of Egypt on 2nd July. Within hours, Napoleon had marched the eight miles to Alexandria, and had occupied the city for the loss of 200 men wounded.

Napoleon set up a French garrison in Alexandria and then set out for Cairo, some 120 miles to the south east. For two weeks the French army struggled through the desert, during the hottest season, plagued by thirst, dysentery, black flies and scorpions. On 21st July they emerged from their ordeal to find the Egyptian army drawn up before them beneath the Pyramids at Giza. This army consisted of 16,000 soldiers spear-headed by an élite cavalry of 8,000 Mamelukes under the command of the ruler of Egypt, the Circassian, Murad Bey.

Napoleon had virtually no cavalry of his own; he did, however, have infantry and guns. On the morning of the battle, he made a speech to his troops. Pointing to the three pyramids towering above them he began:

'Soldiers, from the height of these pyramids, forty-centuries look down upon you !'

The Battle of the Pyramids was a rout. Although the Mamelukes were crack soldiers and horsemen whose lives were dedicated to fighting, they could not hope to over-come the French guns and bayonets. The Egyptian infantry, which had never faced heavy guns before, panicked and fled. In less than two hours Napoleon had destroyed or captured most of the Egyptian army together with the Mameluke cavalry. Murad Bey escaped with only a handful of men.

On 25th July Napoleon entered Cairo and declared Turkish rule at an end. However, his satisfaction was to be short-lived. On 7th August the Battle of the Nile was fought in Aboukir Bay. The British fleet under the command of Nelson destroyed thirteen out of seventeen French warships and mounted a blockade of Egypt. Napoleon and his 55,000 men were cut off, unable to receive supplies and reinforcements from France.

On the morning when he received the news from Aboukir Bay, Napoleon went into breakfast with his officers, observing:

'It seems you like this country. That is very lucky, for we now have no fleet to carry us back to Europe.'

Napoleon's Egyptian Expedition lasted for another year. In July 1799 he received news from Europe, the first he had had in six months. It gave him cause for considerable alarm. France now had not only Britain for an enemy, but Austria, Russia, Naples and Turkey also. She was on the verge of economic collapse; there was talk of restoring the monarchy. Napoleon decided that his only course was to run the British blockade, to make his way back to France, to 'the spot where (he) could be of most use'. Accordingly, on 23rd August 1799, he left his army in Egypt and sailed for France.

The fourteen months that Napoleon spent in Egypt set in motion the scientific examination of its antiquities which laid the foundations of modern Egyptology. In August 1798 Napoleon founded an institute in Cairo based on the Institut de France in Paris to coordinate the researches of the 150 'learned civilians' who had accompanied his army to Egypt. He made the mathematician, Gaspard Monge, president, and he himself became vice-president. The Cairo Institute met every five days, and Napoleon spent so much time there that his officers became jealous and spoke contemptuously of the scholars, calling them 'Pekinese dogs', inferring that they were merely Napoleon's lap-dogs. Napoleon was already a member of the Paris Institute's mathematical section; his Egyptian studies therefore had a mathematical bent.

The 'Pekinese dogs' undertook a variety of projects. Berthollet studied the natron lakes in the Western Desert and the manufacture of indigo; Villoteau studied Arab music; Larrey ophthalmia. Savigny discovered an unknown species of water-lily. Saint-Hilaire made detailed studies of the ostrich and crocodile; and of the polypterus, a species of Nile fish peculiar to that river. Through his study of mummified ibises, Saint-Hilaire became the first man to follow the development of a species through several thousand years. By means of his work on comparative anatomy he paved the way for Darwin.

It was the work of the Academician, Dominique-Vivant Denon, which had the most far-reaching effects. Denon had come to Egypt as a draughtsman. He was fifty years old and had led an eventful life. During a career as a diplomat, his posts had ranged from secretary at the French Embassy at St Petersburg, where he was reputed to be a lover of Catherine the Great, to an assignment in Switzerland, where he was often a guest of Voltaire, and where he had painted the famous 'Breakfast at Ferney'.

During the French Revolution, Denon lived in penury in the slums of Paris, selling his drawings. Eventually, he came to the attention of Jacques Louis David, the great painter. He was given work as David's engraver and was rehabilitated. Denon then achieved some success as an author when he wrote a classic short love story, 'Le point de lendemain'; and an even greater success when he produced the 'Oeuvre priapique', a collection of pornographic etchings.

Before the Revolution, Denon had been a favourite of Madame de Pompadour; after it he became a protégé of Josephine Beauharnais, who recommended him to Napoleon for the Egyptian Expedition. Denon's talent for drawing enabled him to play a vital role in the history of Egyptology.

From the moment Denon set foot in Egypt, he fell in love with all things Egyptian. When General Desaix set off for Upper Egypt in pursuit of the defeated Mameluke leader Murad Bey, Denon went with him. Desaix chased Murad Bey as far as Aswan, some 600 miles south of Cairo, and defeated and killed him at the Battle of Sediman. All the time, Denon sketched away, 'mostly on my knee or standing, even on horseback, and without finishing even one as I should have liked'.

Denon made hundreds of sketches of the antiquities of Ancient Egypt, from the Step Pyramid at Sakkara to the tombs and temples of Thebes; from the temples of Dendera and Edfu to the chapel of Amenophis III at Aswan. Denon's sketch of this chapel is the only one extant; the building itself was pulled down in 1822.

Denon could not fail to notice that many of the monuments he sketched were covered with inscriptions, strange, beautiful, pictorial writings—hieroglyphs. Nobody in Desaix's army could tell him what these hieroglyphs were, or what they meant. Nevertheless, he took pains to copy, as accurately as possible, what he saw. Meantime, other members of Napoleon's group of 'learned civilians' were busy copying inscriptions from

Egyptian monuments; so much so that they ran out of pencils and Conté had to improvise new ones by melting down lead bullets into holders made from the reeds which grew along the banks of the Nile. The 'learned civilians' did not understand the hieroglyphic signs any better than Denon. However, they consulted the ancient Greek writers and decided, erroneously, that the Greeks had been correct in their belief that Ancient Egyptian was basically the same language as Chinese.

By chance, the key to unlocking the secret of Egyptian hieroglyphs was discovered by an insignificant French soldier named d'Hautpoul. In August 1799 a gang of men, under the direction of an engineer-officer named Bouchard, were working in the ruins of Fort Rashid near Rosetta, a coastal town some forty-three miles to the east of Alexandria. D'Hautpoul dug up a piece of black basalt, 3′ 9″ long by 2′ 4½″ wide, one side of which was covered with columns of inscriptions. There was a damaged section containing fourteen lines of the usual mysterious hieroglyphs; thirty-two lines of an even stranger form of writing (later found to be demotic—see page 39); and fifty-four lines of Greek.

Luckily, the importance of the Rosetta Stone, as d'Hautpoul's piece of basalt came to be known, was recognised immediately; Bouchard had it taken to Cairo for further study.

In July 1799 the most important session of the Cairo Institute was held. The savant, Lancret, announced 'the discovery at Rosetta of some inscriptions that may offer much interest'. Lancret had read the Greek inscription on the Rosetta Stone. He revealed that it was a decree issued by the priests of Memphis to commemorate the coronation of Ptolemy V, Epiphanes in 196 B.C. It was reasonable to suppose that the inscriptions written in the other two scripts contained the same text. It was understood that these scripts were Ancient Egyptian, with one, the hieroglyphic, being the formal script, and the other, the demotic, being the cursive script 'of the people' or 'of the country', which is what the word demotic means. The hieroglyphic script was perhaps more accurate than the demotic. Therefore, by comparing the Greek text with the hieroglyphic version, it should be possible to arrive at a decipherment of the hieroglyphs.

Plaster copies of the Rosetta Stone were sent to Paris. Soon, scholars in Germany, Italy, England and France were at work on the task of deciphering the hieroglyphs. All to no avail. Each scholar started from false premises, based on ideas propounded by ancient Greek writers who thought that each hieroglyph had a symbolic meaning. Finally, Silvestre de Sacy announced that hieroglyphs remained 'untouched as the Holy Ark of the Covenant'. Further, 'the problem is too complicated, scientifically insoluble'.

France's hold on Egypt did not long survive the departure of Napoleon in 1799. By 1801, the French had been defeated by both the Turks and the British ; the remnants of Napoleon's expeditionary force to Egypt were repatriated. Many items from their collection of Egyptian antiquities, including the Rosetta Stone, were handed over to the British. General Hutchinson arranged for their transportation to England where George III instructed that they be housed in the British Museum.

The 'learned civilians' who stayed behind in Egypt after Napoleon's departure continued with their work as best they could until they, too, were returned to France.

By 1804, Egypt was under the rule of a man who had been sent to Egypt by the Turkish Government to fight the French, an Albanian soldier of fortune named Mehemet Ali. He retained the link with France, thus enabling French scientists to influence the development of Egyptian scholarship. He also began to modernise the country ; one of the results of his modernisation was the opening up of Egypt to Egyptologists. Mehemet Ali knew nothing about Ancient Egypt, and cared less, but if it amused foreigners to come to Egypt and study the monuments, he was willing to allow it for the sake of good relations with foreign governments.

By 1806, Napoleon's 'Pekinese dogs' were much reduced in number. Of the original band of scholars who had accompanied Napoleon to Egypt, five had been killed in battle, five assassinated, one had been drowned, ten had died of plague and five of dysentery, and five had died in France from the effects of their Egyptian experience. Many had impaired health, their eyesight being especially badly affected due to sun, sand and dust, not to mention the flies which spread the eye diseases which were endemic amongst the Egyptian populace.

Those who remained, however, set to work to publish the discoveries they had made in Egypt. In 1802, Vivant Denon published his 'Journey in Upper and Lower Egypt'.

Between 1809 and 1813, Francois Jomard published his great work, 'Descriptions of Egypt', based on the work of the Institute which Napoleon had founded in Cairo and making full use of Denon's superb drawings. Thus scholars everywhere gained access to all the discoveries made to date in Egypt. Laymen had a new world opened up to them, a world they had never glimpsed before, unlike anything they had ever known. Public interest in the fascinating science of Egyptology had begun.

One major mystery remained. If the history of Ancient Egypt were ever to be known, if Egypt were ever to be seen through the eyes of the Ancient Egyptians themselves, then the secret of hieroglyphs must be unravelled.

Chapter II

THE DECIPHERMENT OF HIEROGLYPHS

The earliest hieroglyphic inscriptions in Egypt go back to at least 3100 B.C. This same script lived on into the Christian era; the latest known hieroglyphic inscription is found on the island of Philae, near Aswan, and is dated to 24th August, A.D. 394, in the reign of the Roman Emperor, Theodosius. By the fifth-century A.D., the understanding of hieroglyphs had been lost altogether.

When Alexander the Great conquered Egypt in 323 B.C., hieroglyphs had for some time been used almost exclusively for inscriptions carved on temple walls or public monuments; they were understood by a rapidly diminishing number of people, mostly priests. Hence the Greeks who ruled Egypt after Alexander called them 'sacred' (Greek: hieros) 'sculptures' (Greek: glupho), from which we derive the term 'hieroglyphs'.

Greek writers such as Herodotus, Strabo and Diodorus, who visited Egypt, all referred to hieroglyphs as a form of picture writing which was completely unintelligible. In the fourth-century A.D., Horapollo, who was perhaps a Hellenised Egyptian, made a survey of Egyptian writing, and published a list of nearly 200 hieroglyphs, with his interpretation of their meaning, in his 'Hieroglyphica'. He established a tradition which was followed by later writers, notably those of the Renaissance onwards, who had access to a manuscript of Horapollo's work which was found early in the fifteenth-century. They all looked for a symbolic meaning for each hieroglyphic sign. They expected a picture of three wavy lines to mean water, and only water; a picture of a head to mean a head, that of an owl to mean an owl, and so on. They made no allowance for the fact that such pictures may, in fact, be phonograms (sound signs), or, indeed, letters of an alphabet rather than pictographs.

The symbolic interpretation of hieroglyphs was further elaborated by the theory that they had an allegorical meaning founded on traditional Egyptian stories and philo-sophies. This belief led to some very fanciful translations. Horapollo, for example, pointed out that the picture of a vulture stood for the word 'mother'. This is correct; the Egyptian word for mother is *mwt* (pronounced 'moot') and is, in this case, represented by a *phonogram*. That is, the word for vulture is the same as that meaning mother; hence the picture of a vulture is used to denote 'mother' because both words have the *same sound*. Horapollo, however, did not recognise this fact. His explanation was that the picture of a vulture was in this instance used in a metaphorical way to represent the idea of motherhood because, he believed, only female vultures existed and they were able to reproduce without the aid of males.

The purely ideographic and symbolic interpretation of hieroglyphic writing prevented any true decipherment being made. It did not, however, prevent many fanciful, but completely erroneous, versions of hieroglyphic texts being put forward.

The most famous of these interpretations was published between 1652 and 1654 by the Jesuit, Athanasius Kircher, in his 'Oedipus Aegyptiacus'. Kircher was professor of mathematics in the University of Rome. His interests were many and varied. He was adept at music, geology, astronomy, and was a competent philologist. He took a special interest in the language that was used in the liturgy of the Christian Church in Egypt, Coptic.

Having made a study of Coptic manuscripts brought back to Europe by an Italian nobleman named Pietro della Valle, Kircher compiled the first Coptic grammar to be published in Europe. His great contribution to the decipherment of hieroglyphs lies in his recognition that the Coptic language was the direct descendant of the language of Egypt spoken in Pharaonic times. Working back from the Coptic is still an important aid to the study of the earlier stages of the native language of Egypt. Kircher, however, was interested in the script which had been used to write down the language of Ancient Egypt—hieroglyphic. He professed to have found the key to its decipherment. The translations which he published in 'Oedipus Aegyptiacus' were based on the by then traditional theory that all Egyptian hieroglyphs had a symbolic meaning. Although Kircher genuinely believed that his understanding of Egyptian philosophy was so perfect that it enabled him to produce a viable translation, his interpretations of the texts, ingenious as they were, were nonsense.

It might be expected that the discovery of the Rosetta Stone in 1799 would have put an end to speculation about the correct way in which to read hieroglyphs. This was not so. The Stone sparked off a spate of attempts to decipher hieroglyphs; but most of them were as fanciful as all such attempts in the past had been. Many interpretations were placed on them, from quotations from the Bible, to astrological and religious doctrines, to excerpts from Chaldean, Hebrew and even Chinese literature. J-F. Champollion realised the absurdity of such ideas and remarked: 'It was as if the Egyptians had nothing to express in their own language.'

Three men, one French, the others Scandinavian, must be given the credit for putting scholars onto the right lines regarding the decipherment of hieroglyphs. First, the Frenchman, J. de Guignes, recognised that some groups of hieroglyphic signs had determinatives, that is, signs which determine the meaning of the foregoing hieroglyphs. Second, G. Zoëga arrived at the conclusion that many hieroglyphs represented the letters of an alphabet. Zoëga also put forward an idea that was later to prove vitally important, the idea that the cartouches, that is, the elongated oval shapes, ⊂===⊃ , which are thought to represent loops of rope, and which are found in many inscriptions, contained royal names. We now know that the cartouche (a French word meaning a scroll or tablet designed to take an inscription) was called 'shenou' by the Egyptians, and signified everything that was encircled by the sun. The cartouche, therefore, shows that the king whose name is written inside it is monarch of all that the sun surveys. Third, J. D. Åkerblad, a Swedish diplomat, compared the Greek and demotic texts on the Rosetta Stone, and identified all the proper names which occur in both texts. He was thus able to publish his version of a demotic alphabet in 1802 in his 'Lettre à M. de Sacy'. He got no further with his studies because he mistakenly believed that the demotic system of writing was entirely alphabetic.

The next great step was taken by Thomas Young, the eminent English scientist. In 1814 he obtained a copy of the Rosetta Stone and from this he achieved some outstanding results in deciphering the demotic section of the Stone. He realised that the demotic system of writing was closely connected with the hieroglyphic. Further, he proved that although some demotic signs represented letters of an alphabet, others did not.

Turning to the Greek section, Young noticed that many words were repeated several times. Working from this basis, he divided the demotic section into its component words. Eventually, he was able to form a Greek-Demotic vocabulary of eighty-six groups of words, most of them correct. He went on to study material other than the Rosetta Stone. But he was hindered in his progress because he was not a philologist and because he did not have sufficient knowledge of Coptic, the language that was to prove an invaluable aid to the decipherment of hieroglyphs.

The man who finally solved the mystery of hieroglyphs was Jean-François Champollion. He was born nine years before the discovery of the Rosetta Stone, on 23rd December 1790, in the French town of Figeac in the Dauphiné, the son of a bookseller who already had a twelve-year-old son, Jacques-Joseph.

The younger of the Champollion brothers first heard the name 'Egypt' at the age of seven when his brother, Jacques-Joseph, a gifted philologist, tried and failed to join Napoleon's Expedition to Egypt.

In 1801, Jacques-Joseph took his eleven-year-old brother to Grenoble, in order to take charge of his education. François showed a precocious talent for Latin, Greek and Hebrew.

In the same year, François visited the home of Jean-Baptiste Fourier, a mathematician and physicist who had been on the Egyptian Expedition. Fourier showed the younger Champollion his collection of Egyptian antiquities. When Champollion saw the hieroglyphs, he asked: 'Can anyone read them?' When he was told 'No' he announced: 'I am going to do it. In a few years I will be able to—when I am big.' From then on, his studies were all directed towards enabling him to fulfil his promise.

By the time Champollion was thirteen years old, he had begun to learn several oriental languages, including Arabic and Coptic. Coptic was his great love. He knew that it was an Egyptian language that was written in Greek characters; and that it had been spoken and written in Egypt, especially by the Christian Egyptians, from about the third- to the sixteenth-century A.D. In Champollion's day, it was understood by some of the priests of the Coptic Church which still flourished in parts of Egypt. Champollion was convinced, correctly, that Coptic was really a late form of that same Egyptian language which was concealed in the hieroglyphs. By the age of sixteen, Champollion spoke and read Coptic so well that he kept journals in it.

The eclectic Champollion next took up the study of Old Chinese, Persian and Parsi.

By 1807, he had prepared his Historical Chart of Ancient Egypt. This was drawn entirely from Biblical references, Latin, Hebrew and Arabic texts, supplemented by Coptic. The seventeen-year-old Champollion presented his paper 'Egypt under the Pharaohs' to the teaching staff of the Lycée at Grenoble. He was immediately made a member of the faculty.

Champollion first saw a copy of the Rosetta Stone in Fourier's house in Grenoble. In 1808, he obtained a copy of the Stone which had been made from the original which was, and is, housed in the British Museum. His initial attempt at decipherment led him to find values for several letters. His satisfaction at such a good beginning was short-lived. News reached him that hieroglyphs had been deciphered by Alexandre Lenoir. However, as soon as Champollion had obtained a copy of Lenoir's 'Nouvelle Explication', he realised that Lenoir's theories were sheer invention.

Champollion continued to work on the Rosetta Stone. It was known already from Zoëga's work that the cartouches on the Stone contained royal names. Åkerblad had identified the name Ptolemaios (Ptolemy to us) in the Greek and demotic sections. Champollion, looking for the name Ptolemaios in the hieroglyphic section, found:

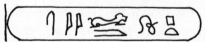

on the sixth line.

By assuming that the name in this cartouche was to be read alphabetically, with each hieroglyph representing a separate letter; and by reading the hieroglyphs, like the demotic, from right to left, Champollion arrived at the reading p-t-o-l-m-y-s, which he took to be the approximation in Egyptian to the Greek Ptolemaios ($\pi\tau o\lambda\epsilon\mu\alpha\iota o\epsilon$).

He was thus able to draw up a tentative sign list, turning the hieroglyphs into his own, Roman, alphabet, as follows:

□ = p
◠ = t
𓊪 = o
𓃭 = l
➡ = m
ϼϼ = y
𓏏 = s

By sheer chance, Champollion was to have the opportunity to confirm his theories. In 1815, Mr W. J. Bankes, a scholar and Member of Parliament who was a friend of the Duke of Wellington, had discovered two red granite obelisks on the island of Philae which had been erected by Ptolemy VIII, Euergetes II and his wife, Kleopatra. One of the obelisks had been badly damaged, only about a third of it remaining. Nevertheless, Bankes arranged for Giovanni Belzoni, the Italian 'antiquarian', to ship both obelisks to Britain, where they were eventually set up on 17th August 1827, in the grounds of Bankes's house at Kingston Lacy in Dorset, on a spot chosen by the Duke of Wellington. Five years before this event, Champollion was given a copy of the inscriptions found in the unbroken Philae obelisk. The shaft of this obelisk was inscribed with hieroglyphs; its base was inscribed in Greek. It was, in effect, a second Rosetta Stone.

When Champollion examined the hieroglyphic inscriptions from the Philae obelisk, he was immediately able to pick out the cartouche bearing the name p-t-o-l-m-y-s (Ptolemaios) which he knew already from the Rosetta Stone. The Greek inscriptions on the obelisk referred also to Kleopatra; and Champollion was able to isolate the relevant cartouche in the hieroglyphic section:

When Champollion made a comparison of the two royal names on the Philae obelisk, he discovered that some of the hieroglyphic characters found in the name Ptolmys (Ptolemaios) looked the same as some of those in the cartouche which he was assuming held the name of Kleopatra (cartouche illustrated above) :

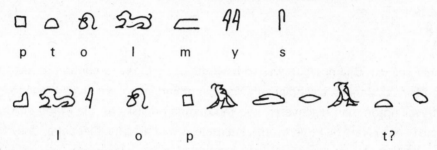

Assuming that pronunciation would be similar to the Greek, he deduced that ⵍ was k, 🦅 was a, ⵍ was d, ○ was r; and that whereas 44 was y, 4 was i. He had two different letters for t—a ⌂ from Ptolemaios, and a ⵍ from Kleopatra. He concluded that they were homophones, that is, equally valid symbols for the same sound, like f and ph in English.

Young had already observed that the signs ⌂○ always occurred at the ends of the names of goddesses and queens. Therefore the ⌂○ at the end of the name Kleopatra was simply a divine, feminine ending. Champollion was able to make a transliteration of the cartouche as follows :

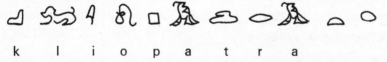

Later it was established that ⵍ is in fact d and that 𝛿ℓ is w, so that the names Ptolemaios and Kleopatra are more correctly transliterated, that is, turned into an approximation of the English alphabet, as Ptwlmys and Kliwpadra, which gives an indication of how the native Egyptians pronounced these foreign (Greek) names.

Champollion went on to test his phonetic approach on as many cartouches as he could find, limiting the field at this stage to those of the Graeco-Roman period. Within months, he had transliterated over 80, amongst which were those of Alexander, Berenice, Tiberius, Domitian and Trajan. His sign list grew apace.

A doubt remained. Would his system, which worked so well for the Graeco-Roman period, be equally effective when applied to the cartouches of an earlier age? Or did the Egyptians only use hieroglyphs phonetically when dealing with foreign names?

In September 1822 Champollion received copies of reliefs from a temple which lay between the first and second cataracts of the Nile, a temple which has become famous because of its dramatic rescue from the waters of the reservoir behind the High Dam at Aswan, the temple of Abu Simbel. Examining the cartouches, Champollion found one which read:

He knew already that ⌐ was the sound s; he had given the value of m to the sign 𝕄 (actually, it is ms). The sign ☉ was obviously meant to be the sun; in Coptic, the word for sun is *re*. Putting all this information together, he came up with a reading for the signs in the right-hand side of the cartouche. ☉𝕄⌐⌐ might be made up of a phonogram (that is, a sign representing a sound) ☉ meaning re, and several alphabetic signs, and might, therefore, be read re-m-s-s. The name of the Pharaoh, Ramesses (sometimes spelled Rameses), mentioned in the Bible, flashed across his mind.

But what about the signs on the left-hand side of the cartouche, 𝄞 ? According to his alphabetic list, 𝄞 was i and ⬭ was mn. Therefore, he deduced, 𝄞 might mean the name of the god, Amun. As for the sign ⨝: he knew from the Greek that a king was often said to be 'beloved of' a god. In Coptic, 'to love' is *me* or *mere*; perhaps ⨝ was to be read mr (pronounced 'mer') and mean 'beloved'. The left-hand side of the cartouche would therefore be read mr imn and mean 'beloved of Amun'.

Champollion went on to another cartouche,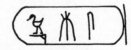

The bird on the left-hand side of this cartouche is an ibis, sacred to the god, Thoth. It is followed by two signs, 𝕄 and ⌐ to which Champollion has assigned the values m and s.

The name in this cartouche must surely be Thoth-m-s or Thothmes, known from Greek records to have been a Pharaoh (Tuthmosis to the Greeks).

Champollion had made a major breakthrough. The secret of Egyptian writing was that it combined signs representing sounds with signs representing ideas. He felt that he was now able to publish his results. On 29th September 1822, at the age of thirty-two, he read his memorable paper, 'Lettre à M. Dacier relative à l'alphabet des hièroglyphes phonétique', to the Members of the Academy in Paris, and won immortal fame.

In his letter to M. Dacier, Champollion made no mention of his discoveries concerning the decipherment of the names of Ramesses and Thothmes (Tuthmosis). He waited until 1824 to publish these in his 'Précis du système hièroglyphic'. He also failed to mention any debt he might owe to the work of others, notably Åkerblad and Young.

The work of decipherment went on. Lepsius and Brugsch in Germany, de Rougé in France, Rosellini in Italy all made their contributions. Champollion himself at long last made a visit to Egypt in 1828-1829, interpreting and deciphering. He died three years later, on 4th March 1832 : he was only forty-one years old.

Chapter III

HOW WRITING BEGAN: INTRODUCTION

The modern system of writing, that is, the system of breaking down the spoken word into its component parts, consisting of vowels and consonants, and representing each of the sounds thus arrived at by alphabetic signs, is very artificial. To the mind of prehistoric man it would have been impossible to grasp.

Prehistoric men could comprehend pictures of objects and animals; they could understand that a picture of an animal painted upon a cave wall represented a real animal—a not inconsiderable intellectual achievement. It can be seen from cave paintings at sites such as Lascaux in France and Altamira in Spain that as far back as 25,000 years ago, prehistoric men used cave paintings in their magic ceremonies. Painting an animal on a cave wall, and transfixing it with painted arrows, was apparently an attempt by prehistoric men to gain power over the animal and make it vulnerable to the hunters. The painting of an animal had taken the place of the real animal for magical purposes.

The earliest known writing was based on a simple idea. By means of simplified drawings, known to us as *pictographs*, the men who invented writing wrote down symbols which represented words in their language. Thus, a picture of a fish ⟠ denoted a fish, a picture of a face ♈ denoted a face, and so on. Today, the Chinese and Japanese still base their written language on this system. In Ancient China, the drawing ⊙ represented the sun, and ☽ the moon. In modern Chinese, these symbols have been stylised into the characters 日 and 月. There are a vast number of signs in a pictographic system of writing such as the Chinese; written Chinese is thus extremely difficult to learn.

C

A pictographic system of writing has further obvious limitations. Simple picto-graphs can serve to represent concrete objects, but they cannot express actions or abstract concepts such as the verb 'to think'.

This problem can be solved by the use of *ideograms*, that is, symbols which stand for several related words or concepts. Ideograms, therefore, are *sense signs*. In order to represent a physical action, for instance, a picture can be drawn of a certain stage in that action: for example, a picture of a man carrying a basket on his head ⚱ could mean 'to carry'; similarly, ⚡ could mean 'to fall'; ⚱ could mean 'to think'. The original pictograph ⊙ meaning 'sun' can be extended into an ideogram meaning 'day' or 'daytime'. The pictograph of a mouth ⚬ can be used to indicate the actions of the mouth—speaking, kissing etc. The sign ⚬ foot can denote the verbs 'to go' or 'to stand'. The meaning of each ideogram has to be judged according to context.

Picture writing which consists entirely of pictographs and ideograms can be very simple, universally understood no matter what language or alphabet the reader of the sign normally uses. For example, a picture of a man ⚱ would be read as *homme* in French, *hombre* in Spanish, *uomo* in Italian; but the meaning of the sign would be the same for everyone.

Today, universally understood pictographs have been put to good use in many ways. The picture of a man on the door of a public convenience ensures that no woman will enter; there is no need for notices saying 'men only' in many different languages to be posted. Signs saying 'Beware of wild animals' or 'Beware of cattle' can only be under-stood by someone who reads English. But international road signs bearing the *picto-*

graphs or can be understood by everyone. However, international

road signs do sometimes illustrate that the use of pictographs is not without its

problems. Does the sign mean 'It is very windy; umbrellas are liable to be

blown inside out' or does it mean 'Road works'.

Ideograms and pictographs have serious limitations. They can be extremely am-
biguous. How, for instance, is one to decipher the following message:

Here we see a simplified picture of a man with his hand to his mouth (an ideogram
denoting an action of some sort). He is pointing towards a tent (a pictograph denoting
a concrete object). Does the picture mean 'I am hungry and I'm going into my tent to
eat'? Or is the man yawning, and, politely covering his mouth with his hand, saying:
'I am tired. I am going into my tent to sleep'? Or is he cupping his hand to his mouth and
shouting: 'Help! My tent is on fire'? Or is he shrugging his shoulders and complaining:
'My mother-in-law came into my tent an hour ago and she hasn't stopped talking since'?

The story is told of a king who received a message showing the pictures of a bird, a
mouse, a frog and five arrows. It is to be hoped that he interpreted the message
correctly, for it meant: 'Can you fly like a bird, hide in the ground like a mouse, leap
through the marshes like a frog? If not, avoid war with us for we shall defeat you with
our arrows.'

The solution to the problem of ambiguity in picture writing lies in the transition of
such writing from the *purely pictorial* representation of *concrete objects* to the *artificial*
representation of *sounds*. Hence the term *phonogram*, or sound sign, is used to
describe this more advanced development in picture writing.

Phonograms make use of the principle of rebus or charade. That is, they use pictures of
things not to represent the things themselves but to indicate something entirely
different which perhaps is not easy to put into pictographs, but which chances to have
the same or a similar sound as an easily-pictured thing.

Children today sometimes send each other coded messages using the rebus or
'play on words' system. For instance, the English verb 'I saw' can be rendered, to an
English-speaking person, by the picture of an eye placed next to the picture of a
carpenter's saw: 👁 ⌐ . Similarly, a picture of a bee 🐝 can be placed next to the
picture of a leaf 🍃 ; the resulting picture-word, to be pronounced 'bee-leaf', is

spelled differently yet possesses the same sound as the noun 'belief', and can therefore be used to denote that word.

An essential difference between pictographs and phonograms is that whereas pictographs can be universally understood regardless of the language spoken by the writer or reader of the pictograph, phonograms can only be understood by speakers of the language which is used to make up the 'play on words' which produces the phonogram. A phonogram playing on French words will make no sense to a non-French-speaker; just as a phonogram playing on German words will not make sense to someone who does not speak German.

A pictographic system of writing is, of course, not nearly so convenient to use as an *alphabetic* system, that is, a system in which each of a minimum number of signs denotes one simple sound in a language.

Today, most western European languages, including English, are written in the *Roman alphabet*, which has 26 letters. The basic Roman alphabet is not large enough to accommodate all the sounds in some of these languages; accent marks have had to be added to some letters in order to show differences in pronunciation. In French, for example, accented letters include é, è, à, ç; in German, ä and ö. In some languages, extra letters have been added to the original twenty-six-letter Roman alphabet—the German ß (=ss) and the Danish ø, for example. Other languages use a Roman alphabet of less than twenty-six letters. Serbo-Croat has no q, w, x and y; the Hawaiian language uses only twelve letters. Gaelic is written in an alphabet of eighteen letters which is derived from the Roman.

There are several alphabets other than the Roman in common use. The *Greek alphabet*, which has twenty-four letters, is used in Greece, and by scientists. The word 'alphabet' comes from its first two letters, A (alpha) and B (beta). The *Cyrillic alphabet* which has thirty-three letters, is used in Russia and other Slavic countries such as Bulgaria. It was adapted from the Greek alphabet in the ninth-century A.D. by St Cyril. He was a Greek priest who, having been sent to convert the Slavs of Bulgaria and Moravia to Christianity, wanted to write the Gospels in their language. The *Hebrew alphabet* has twenty-two letters.

There are twenty-eight letters in the *Arabic alphabet*. The spread of Islam from the seventh-century A.D. onwards imposed it on a variety of languages other than Arabic, from Persian, an Aryan language, to Turkish, a Tatar language, to Hindustani, an Aryan language spoken in parts of India.

The classical language of India is written in an alphabet which has characters for fourteen vowels and thirty-three simple consonants, plus two further symbols. This *Sanskrit*, or *Devanagari alphabet*, is a well-constructed one in which every letter has one invariable sound. This is in contrast to the English alphabet. It is estimated that there are forty-two sounds in English; we have only twenty-six letters to represent them.

Some languages use two alphabets. Serbo-Croat is written in the Cyrillic alphabet in one part of Yugoslavia, and in the Roman alphabet in another. Occasionally, it is decided to change from one alphabet to another. This happened in Turkey, in 1928, when the Turks changed from using the Arabic alphabet to using the Roman alphabet because their ruler, Kemal Ataturk, considered that this would be an advantage to a country striving to enter the modern European world. New alphabets can be introduced—the Initial Teaching Alphabet is a phonetic alphabet designed to help English-speaking children to read.

Although the advantages of an alphabetic system of writing may seem obvious to us, it should be remembered that this was not the case with many peoples, ancient and modern (for example, the Chinese, who still do not use an alphabetic system). In fact, such a system took many centuries to evolve.

European languages use an alphabet which is descended from the Greek either directly or via the Roman alphabet which itself was derived from the Greek. The Greeks, however, did not invent the alphabet. At the beginning of the ninth-century B.C. they took it over ready-made from the Phoenicians. The Phoenicians themselves were merely using a variation of the writing used at that time by the Semites of Syria-Palestine—Canaanite writing. The names of the Canaanite letters, *'alef* (which means ox), *beth* (house), *gimel* (camel), *daleth* (door) etc. were adapted by the Greeks into *alpha*, *beta*, *gamma*, *delta* etc. The Canaanite letters were originally pictographs, with '*alef* being represented by the picture of an ox's head, *beth* by a simplified drawing of a house etc. From Canaanite the Semitic alphabets such as Hebrew and Arabic are descended.

The earliest known version of the Canaanite alphabet is thought to have been developed about 1800 B.C. In A.D. 1917, Sir Alan Gardiner was working on material from the site of an Ancient Egyptian temple, dedicated to the goddess Hathor, at Serâbît el-Khâdim in the Sinai peninsula. Eleven of the inscriptions on which he was working resembled Egyptian hieroglyphs, but were not Egyptian. Gardiner came to the conclusion that in these inscriptions lay the nucleus of an alphabetic system, which he called 'proto-Semitic'. He put forward the theory that the inventor of this rudimentary alphabet must have been a Semite, rather than an Egyptian. This theory he based on two facts. First, the goddess Hathor is called, in the Sinai inscription, *Ba'lat*, which is a Semitic term. Second, according to inscriptions at the site, when the turquoise mines at Serâbît el-Khâdim were exploited in Dynasty XII, Semites were employed there, mostly as miners. Hence, Gardiner came to the conclusion that his 'proto-Semitic' alphabet, from which all other alphabets are descended, was invented by a Semite, probably in the reign of the Twelfth Dynasty King of Egypt, Amenemmes III (*c.* 1842-1797 B.C.).

Although the 'proto-Semitic' alphabet was developed under the aegis of the Egyptians, as it were, they themselves did not adopt the new invention. They continued as they had begun, with the much more cumbersome non-alphabetic system of writing which they had received from the Mesopotamians nearly 1,500 years before.

How writing began: Mesopotamia

Mesopotamia lay in the plain between the two rivers, Tigris and Euphrates, roughly within the borders of modern Iraq. By 4000 B.C. southern Mesopotamia was inhabited by a race of farmers who had migrated from the north. These farmers, who were to be an important civilising force in the Near East, are known as Ubaidians, from an excavation carried out about fifty years ago at one of their settlements near the ancient city of Ur, Tell al-Ubaid.

Around the end of the fifth-millenium B.C., hordes of Semitic nomads from the Syrian desert and the Arabian peninsula began to infiltrate the settlements of the non-Semitic Ubaidians. The subsequent cross-fertilisation of the two cultures laid the foundations of a new era in Mesopotamia.

About 3500 B.C., a third group of people arrived in Mesopotamia, possibly from Central Asia via Iran—the Sumerians. They were the builders of the world's first civilisation. In the next 1,200 years, the Sumerians reached unprecedented heights of achievement in art and architecture, social and political organisation, and religion, in creating an urban, literate society in southern Mesopotamia—Sumer.

In 2300 B.C., the Sumerian civilisation came under the dominance of Sargon the Great, a Semite. He was the first ruler to unite Sumer with the northern half of Mesopotamia. This unified nation he ruled from a new city, Agade, which he built in a part of south-central Mesopotamia called Akkad. The Semitic language that was used in Mesopotamia from Sargon's time onwards is called Akkadian. It became the *lingua franca* of the ancient world.

The greatest achievement of the Sumerian civilisation was the invention of writing. Economic necessity seems to have been the mother of this invention, for as their civilisation became more prosperous and more complicated, the Sumerians found that it was essential that some record be kept of temple and palace property.

The form and method of writing arose out of conditions in Mesopotamia. The purpose of the writing was to record items of property such as cattle, jars of wine, sacks of grain. Hence the writing took the form of simplified pictures of such items—pictographs.

The method of writing was influenced by the materials available. Stone was scarce; papyrus and paper unknown; clay was plentiful between the Tigris and the Euphrates. And so the first writing was done on wet clay moulded into small slabs known as tablets, with a 'pen' or stylus made from a reed whittled to a sharp point. When the writing was finished, the clay tablet was left to dry and harden in the sun. The pointed stylus was soon discarded in favour of a stylus with a triangular tip, which was pressed down into the clay, leaving wedge-shaped impressions in it—*cuneiform writing.*

The earliest known examples of Mesopotamian writing were found at Uruk, a site in southern Mesopotamia near the city of al-Ubaid. Uruk has eighteen stratigraphical levels; at level IV, which can be dated to about 3500 B.C., were found small tablets inscribed with pictographs of objects such as cows, sheep and cereals, scratched on the surface of the tablet with a pointed reed. Each object is accompanied by a series of signs shaped like strokes, circles and semicircles, presumably numerals. The purpose of the 'writing' on the Uruk IV tablets is uncertain, but probably is of an economic nature.

For the next 500 years or so, it seems that writing was confined to the use to which it had been put during the Uruk IV period.

At about 3000 B.C., Sumerian writing underwent a change, both in content and in style and method. On the earliest tablets, the pictographs were scratched haphazardly onto the surface; no attempt seems to have been made to put the signs into columns, either vertical or horizontal. Later, the pictographs were set down in vertical columns, usually beginning at the top right-hand corner of the tablet.

By about 3250 B.C., the scribes had discovered that there was a tendency to smudge the text with their hands if they wrote in vertical columns. And so writing in vertical columns gave way to texts written horizontally, from left to right, top to bottom of the tablet The pictographs themselves underwent a 90° turn. For instance, the sign for 'ox', consisting of a simplified drawing of an ox's head which had been written ⚭ , was now written ⚮ .

At two sites, Jemdat Nasr and Uruk III, dated *c.* 3000 B.C., clay and stone tablets have been found which record lists of personal names (probably wage lists), lists of objects or inventories, plus an assortment of economic texts such as receipts and memoranda. On these tablets, the objects depicted are no longer scratched with a pointed reed. Instead, an obliquely cut reed-stem has been used and pressed down in the wet clay, resulting in the characteristic 'wedges' of cuneiform writing. The pictograph becomes stylised; a scratched picture of an ox's head which used to be written ⚮ is now written ⊐⏐⟩ .

Development of Mesopotamian writing

Original pictograph	Later pictograph	Early cuneiform	Original or derived meaning
			bird
			fish
			ox
			sun, day
			grain
			to stand, to go

The Sumerians went on to develop their writing until they achieved a system of such flexibility that people who spoke quite different languages such as Akkadian, Babylonian and Assyrian were able to adapt cuneiform to their own uses.

With the passage of time, cuneiform writing died out and was replaced by an alphabetic system which was derived from the 'proto-Semitic' alphabet. The meaning of cuneiform script was lost for centuries. However, just as the mystery of Egyptian hieroglyphs was solved in the nineteenth-century thanks to the Rosetta Stone, so the mystery of cuneiform writing was unravelled thanks to its own version of the Rosetta Stone.

Hewn into the face of a mountain in Behistun in Iran is a 1,306-line inscription which was carved on the instructions of Darius the Great, King of Persia, some 2,500 years ago. The inscription is in three languages—Old Persian, Elamite and Akkadian. In the nineteenth-century, scholars were able to translate parts of the Old Persian inscription, and then, by comparing it with the other two, they were able to decipher the Elamite and the Akkadian, and thus 'crack' the cuneiform writing.

Chapter IV

WRITING IN EGYPT

The pre-dynastic Egyptians lived in agricultural communities of an African rather than a western Asiatic character. It seems probable that the late pre-dynastic Egyptians were feeling their way towards an organised urban society, forced to do so by their growing prosperity and by the necessity to deal with the annual Nile flood. Shortly before 3100 B.C. they received a stimulus from outside Egypt. Archaeological evidence points towards Mesopotamia as the source of that stimulus.

Mesopotamian motifs are found in Egyptian art—composite animals, especially winged griffins and serpent-necked felines; pairs of entwined animals. A knife found at Gebel el Arak has a handle depicting, on one side, Mesopotamian-style ships, and on the other, a hero dominating two lions, the hero being dressed in Mesopotamian costume.

In architecture, the late pre-dynastic Egyptians began to use mud-brick when they had previously used reeds, papyrus, palm-branches and rush matting. The façades of their more important buildings were constructed of mud-brick arranged in recesses in the style which was used in Mesopotamia.

The Egyptians of this period used Mesopotamian objects such as cylindrically-shaped seals. Three of the cylinder-seals which have been found in Egypt are thought to date from the Uruk IV period (c. 3500 B.C.). The Mesopotamians used cylinder-seals to impress their 'signatures' on their wet clay tablets. The Egyptians did not have clay tablets; they simply used the seals as amulets.

The most important contribution made by Mesopotamia to early Egyptian civilisation was *writing*. It seems probable that the Sumerians introduced the idea of writing to Egypt shortly before 3100 B.C. The Egyptians immediately adapted Mesopotamian pictographs to Egyptian ones; the first Egyptian hieroglyphic writing, found on slate palettes of late pre-dynastic times, employs pictographs showing Egyptian rather than Mesopotamian objects. It gives the impression of being fully developed at this early stage in Egyptian dynastic history.

The Mesopotamians changed from picture writing to cuneiform script at an early date. They had a tendency toward using abstract symbols from the beginning; cuneiform writing bears little resemblance to the original pictographs. The Egyptians, on the other hand, preferred the concrete rather than the abstract; this is reflected in most of their hieroglyphic signs which are exact illustrations of the objects they depict. As we shall see, hieroglyphic writing was later supplemented by hieratic and demotic scripts. But, typical of the conservative Egyptians, they did not abandon one style of writing for another, and hieroglyphic writing was used from the outset until A.D. 394, when the last-known hieroglyphic inscription in Egypt was carved.

The purposes for which writing was used differed in Mesopotamia and Egypt. The Mesopotamians first used writing in a practical way, for administrative purposes. The Egyptians initially used writing as an adjunct to monumental art. One of the earliest examples of such art is the Narmer palette. This commemorative slate palette is carved with reliefs showing the unification of Egypt under King Narmer, the founder of Dynasty I, *c.* 3100. The top of the palette is decorated with two faces of the cow-headed goddess, Hathor. Between the Hathor heads is written the name of Narmer, using pictographs of the *n'r*-fish and the *mr*-chisel (that is, two phonograms, *n'r-mr*, read Narmer), one of the oldest known specimens of Egyptian writing. The objects depicted in the pictographs are typically Egyptian rather than Mesopotamian.

From its inception in Egypt hieroglyphic writing seems to have consisted of a combination of ideograms (signs representing ideas) and phonograms (signs representing sounds) put together in a fairly complex way. Because phonograms had been introduced into the written language of Ancient Egypt at an early stage, Egyptian hieroglyphic writing from the beginning was more than just simple picture writing.

The phonograms were identical in appearance to ideograms, but their meaning was extended. For instance, the sign ⬭ is the ideogram for *r* (mouth); however, ⬭ (*r*) can also be used as a phonogram. In the Egyptian language, the preposition 'towards' has the same sound as the noun 'mouth' (*r*, pronounced 'ro' in each case). And so both words were represented by the hieroglyph ⌒ . The word for face was *hr* (pronounced 'her') and was written with the sign ♔ . The word for 'on' was also pronounced 'her', and so it, too, was written with the sign ♔ .

In the same way, the word for 'eye' was written ◈ and pronounced 'an'; by the principle of rebus, the eye ◈ came to mean 'beautiful' because the word for beautiful was *an*, and thus had the same sound as *an*, eye. Similarly, the hoe ⌐ (mer) was used for the verb mer, to love; the goose ⌐ (sa) was used to write sa, son; the beetle ⌐ (heper) was used to write heper, become; the lotus ⌐ (ha) was used to write ha, thousand.

In the examples given above, the words for face, eye, hoe, goose, beetle and lotus have been transliterated, that is, written in the Roman alphabet as her, an, mer, sa, heper and ha. From these transliterations it may be supposed that the Egyptians had at least two vowels (a and e). This is not so; the transliterations above have been rendered with vowels in order to indicate pronunciation to the reader.

In common with other Semitic scripts, both ancient and modern, such as Phoenician, Hebrew and Arabic, the Egyptians did *not* indicate vowels in their writing. This phenomenon is explained by the nature of Semitic languages where vowels are used in the *spoken* language simply to indicate modifications in the way groups of consonants, put together to make up words, are pronounced, since the pronunciation of the consonants determines the meaning of the word. The roots of the words, made up of consonants, do not change. It is easy, in these circumstances, to reach the conclusion that consonants are all that matter, that vowels are not important, and so omit vowels in the *written* language. This can sometimes lead to serious misunderstandings; for example, the Arabic word قتل qtl, which can be read 'qatal(a)'—'he killed' or 'qutil(a)'—'he was killed' according to context. The Ancient Egyptians must also have experienced such confusions.

Most words in the Egyptian language were made up of groups of signs representing one, two or three consonants which were written in hieroglyphs in *uniliteral, biliteral* or *triliteral signs*. The written language had twenty-four uniliteral signs each representing one consonant, a kind of 'alphabet' which enabled the Egyptians to avoid using hundreds of other signs. The biliteral signs, by means of which the Egyptians could express two consonants in a single sign, and the triliteral signs, in which one hieroglyph stood for three consonants, also helped to avoid the necessity of using a vast number of signs. The written language had many ideograms and more than 150 phonograms.

Thus Egyptian hieroglyphs were an elaborate script which was capable of indicating phonetically all possible combinations of sounds in the language. The Egyptians never developed the use of their 'alphabetic' signs to the exclusion of all others. Only late on in their history did they display a preference for the use of alphabetic signs when writing royal names (e.g. Ptolemy, Cleopatra), or deliberately archaising inscriptions on public monuments.

The Egyptians used three *forms* of writing during their history. They began with hieroglyphs; out of hieroglyphic writing there developed a more cursive script known as hieratic; and, eventually, out of hieratic, a rapid script known as demotic.

Hieroglyphs or hieroglyphic writing. The words 'hieroglyph' and 'hieroglyphic' are often used interchangeably, and are sometimes used incorrectly to describe the language of Ancient Egypt. Strictly speaking, the word 'hieroglyph' is a noun and should be used to refer to the *writing* of the Ancient Egyptians, or to the writing of any other people who use pictographs. The term 'hieroglyphic' is an adjective and should only be used to describe the mode of writing. Thus, it is correct to say 'I can read hieroglyphs' or 'I can read hieroglyphic writing'; it is incorrect to say 'I can read hieroglyphics'. Neither is it correct to refer to the 'hieroglyphic language'. There is no such thing as a hieroglyphic language; only hieroglyphic writing. As far as Ancient Egypt is concerned, the language is simply called 'the ancient Egyptian language' or 'Ancient Egyptian'.

The term 'hieroglyph' is derived from the Greek words *hieros* (sacred) *glupho* (sculptures), and was so called because by the time the Greeks first saw the writing of Ancient Egypt it was inscribed almost exclusively on the walls of temples and public monuments.

The Ancient Egyptians themselves called their writing 𓆑𓏤𓊹𓏥 *mdw nṯr* ('medoo neter') 'the god's words', the god referred to being Thoth, the god of wisdom who invented writing.

In the beginning, hieroglyphic writing in Egypt was used for all purposes. It was used for religious and monumental inscriptions on the walls of temples and tombs, on stone stelae and on papyrus, on wooden coffins and sarcophagi. It was used for business and administrative documents. On the walls of temples, tombs and public monuments, the decorative effect of the hieroglyphs played an important part; they were often carved in elaborate detail and exquisitely coloured. When hieroglyphs were used on papyrus, however, they were from the outset drawn in a much abbreviated and utilitarian form. The use of hieroglyphs carved in stone persisted throughout Egyptian history, the latest known examples being carved in the Temple of Isis at Philae, and dated to A.D. 394.

Hieroglyphic writing was perfectly satisfactory for use on stone, where it was shaped with precision by a chisel. On papyrus, the use of a reed pen led to hieroglyphs being written rapidly in abbreviated and more rounded forms. Gradually, the use of hieroglyphic writing became more and more confined to stone inscriptions and religious texts written on papyrus. A more cursive script was developed for use on materials other than stone. This script is called *hieratic*.

The word hieratic comes from the Greek *hieratikos*, meaning 'priestly', so called because by the Graeco-Roman period it was the script used almost exclusively by priests. When first introduced, hieratic was very like hieroglyphic writing in appearance. From about 2000 B.C. it had a distinctive style of its own, and was used for any non-religious writing done on papyrus. Hieroglyphs continued to be used for inscriptions on stone; and until about 1000 B.C. for religious texts written on papyrus. After that date, even religious texts on papyrus were written in hieratic.

The third type of script used by the Ancient Egyptians was *demotic*, a term taken from the Greek *demoticos*, meaning popular. Demotic is a very rapid form of hieratic, almost on a par with shorthand; its appearance has been likened to 'a series of agitated commas'. It first came into use about 700 B.C.; by the Graeco-Roman period it was the ordinary writing of everyday life for those people who could write. The majority of the Egyptian populace was illiterate, relying on the services of professional scribes when it came to the reading or writing of letters, business documents or wills.

The scribes

In Ancient Egypt, the task of learning to read and write was not undertaken lightly. The Egyptians did not have the advantage of a wholly alphabetic system of writing. In order to write fluently, an Egyptian needed to learn hundreds of picture signs representing sounds, combinations of sounds, and ideas. The minimum number of hieroglyphic signs needed to write simple sentences is about 200. A list of signs used by a young Egyptian schoolboy has been found; it contains more than 450 characters. At a more advanced stage he would have needed about 750 signs; eventually, a competent scribe would have known several hundred more.

It is not surprising, therefore, that few Egyptians could read or write. The average Egyptian was a peasant farmer with little or no interest beyond the confines of his own village; his energies were expended on growing his crops and tending his animals. He had neither the inclination nor the opportunity, nor, since professional scribes were plentiful, the need, to learn to write.

In an illiterate country such as Egypt, the man who could read and write was considered greatly superior to his fellow men. In a bureaucratic country such as Egypt, the scribe was master. He was a member of a profession which was 'the foremost of all professions'. The office of scribe was the opening to bigger and better things. The great Amenophis, son of Hapu, was scribe to his king, Amenophis III; he reached one of the highest offices to which a noble could aspire, that of Scribe to the King.

The profession of scribe was not the exclusive preserve of the nobility. Even a boy of lowly origin could become a scribe, provided his father could afford to send him to school, or find him a rich sponsor.

Schools were usually attached to temples. Boys were sent there from the age of four or five. They were often boarders, although the school did not provide food. Instead, servants or mothers would have to visit the school daily with bread and beer for the boys. The main subjects taught there were reading, writing, arithmetic, geography and history. The object of education was to train boys to be clerks in local and government offices, to give them sufficient basic knowledge for entry into the priesthood, and to train them to be artists and draughtsmen.

Writing exercises were done on small pieces of stone or broken pottery (potsherds) which were thrown away after use. This habit has proved invaluable to Egyptologists. Sometimes potsherds are found on which a schoolboy has practised writing a well-known story which has come down to us in a damaged version. Thanks to the schoolboy, the Egyptologist is sometimes able to fill in gaps in his knowledge.

One of the most popular exercises a schoolboy had to copy out was an exhortation to him to work hard. This served the dual purpose of improving his writing and subtly working on his mind:

'Persevere every day. Thus shall you obtain mastery over writing. Spend not a day in idleness or you will be beaten. The ear of a boy is on his back—he listens when he is beaten!'

Should a boy be tempted by another way of life, model 'letters' from fathers were often given to him to copy out:

'I am told . . . you set your mind on work in the field, and turn your back on writing. Do you not realise how the husbandman fares when the harvest is registered (for taxation purposes)? The worm has taken half the corn, the hippopotamus has eaten the rest. The mice abound in the field, and the locust has descended. The cattle devour, and the sparrows steal. Woe to the husbandman! But the scribe, he directs the work of everybody. For him there are no taxes, for he pays tribute in writing, and there are no dues for him.'

'What do you mean by saying, "It is thought that the soldier is better off than the scribe"? Let me tell you how woefully the soldier fares. His superiors are many . . . He is woken up after only an hour's sleep. He is driven like an ass. He works until the sun goes down. He is hungry. He is dead while yet alive.'

D

The picture these 'letters' give of the misery endured by men who take up professions other than that of scribe is, of course, biased and exaggerated. Nevertheless, the profession of scribe was the most important one in Egypt. The scribe was the man who moulded Egyptian thought and maintained standards throughout Egyptian history.

'Their names abide forever . . . their names are pronounced because of the books they made. Be a scribe, put it in your heart, that your name might fare likewise. More profitable than a graven tombstone is a book.'

The scribe's materials and tools

The Egyptians used many kinds of material on which to write: stone, wood, metal, parchment, vellum, leather. But the writing material which set them apart from other ancient peoples, and gave them such an advantage, was *papyrus*. Whereas, for instance, the Mesopotamians were forced to used baked clay, which could be cumbersome and heavy, on which to write because they had no other material readily available to them, the Egyptians had the enormous advantage of a light, smooth material, papyrus. Papyrus was made from narrow strips of the pith of fresh green papyrus plant stems. Two layers of strips were placed together at right angles, pressed and pounded into a long flat sheet. Several sheets of papyrus could be joined together to make a roll of papyrus (one such roll is known to be 130' long) or a scroll.

The word papyrus has given us our word paper; paper, however, is made of wood or cotton fibres, and was invented in China. Papyrus plants once grew in profusion in the Nile valley and were used for many purposes other than 'paper' making—for boats, skiffs, ropes, baskets, sandals, fences, mats. A sad fact is that, today, papyrus has disappeared from Egypt. Attempts are being made to grow it in plant nurseries; and the most famous clump is to be found in the courtyard of Cairo Museum.

The Egyptian word for scribe is *sš* ('sesh-es') and means 'he who writes'; it is written 𓏞𓏛𓊹 . The hieroglyphic sign illustrates the three tools of the scribe. First, the palette, usually made of wood or alabaster, with two bowls containing cakes of 'ink'. A scribe's 'ink' took the form of round, dry cakes of colour, usually black or red. On papyrus, the red 'ink' served to highlight rubrics in a sentence; on stone, it was used to correct mistakes in hieroglyphs which had been sketched out in black ready for carving. Second, the pot, containing a light gum. Third, the holder for his 'pens'. The 'pens' were really brushes made from reeds with carefully frayed and trimmed ends. They were moistened every so often with the light gum, brushed across the cake of 'ink' to take up the colour, and applied to the material being used for the writing. A string connected the three tools so that they could be carried in the scribe's hand or slung over his shoulder.

The status in society enjoyed by the scribe is reflected in the fact that many of them could afford to have statues made of themselves; and in the fact that they are proud to have these statues depict them in the characteristic pose of the scribe—seated cross-legged upon the ground, wearing a kilt. The kilt is stretched taut across the knees thus providing a 'desk' on which to rest a papyrus-roll. The face of the scribe in such statues, especially the eyes, has an alert and eager expression as the scribe prepares to 'direct the affairs of everyone'.

Chapter V

THE LANGUAGE OF THE ANCIENT EGYPTIANS

A language normally has affinities with several other tongues which, grouped together, form a 'family'. English, for instance, belongs to the Indo-European family which also includes the languages of modern Russia, ancient Turkey (Hittite) and ancient India (Sanskrit). The Ancient Egyptian language belongs to the so-called Hamito-Semitic family. The term 'Hamitic' refers to the African group of languages. According to Genesis X, one of Noah's sons went forth after the Flood and became the ancestor of the African tribes. From the name of this son, Ham, is the word Hamitic derived. 'Semitic' comes from the name of another of Noah's sons, Shem, who was traditionally the ancestor of the Aramean, Phoenician and Assyrian races; and, ironically, of both the Hebrews and the Arabs.

The origin of the Ancient Egyptian language is not precisely known. It is thought to have elements of the Hamitic group of languages spoken in north-east Africa, such as Berber, Galla and Somali; over 100 Egyptian words have roots in common with words in these Hamitic languages. Ancient Egyptian was also influenced by the Semitic languages; over 300 words have been traced in which the Egyptian word has roots in common with the Semitic.

The linguistic background of Ancient Egyptian is, as far as can be deduced, much the same as its supposed racial origins—a mixture of Semitic and African.

The language of Ancient Egypt should not be confused with that spoken in Egypt today which is, of course, Arabic, the language that was introduced into Egypt after she was conquered by invaders from the Arabian Peninsula, the Muslim Arabs whose religious zeal led them to extend Islam and their empire from A.D. 650 to 850 until they ruled over the whole of northern Africa and the Near East. They conquered Egypt in A.D. 640.

The Egyptians began their written records shortly before 3100 B.C., and continued with the use of hieroglyphs, later supplemented by hieratic and demotic, until the Christian era. Unfortunately, it is only from these written records that we know Ancient Egyptian; we cannot be sure how Egyptian was spoken. Any attempt to reconstruct the sound of Ancient Egyptian is greatly handicapped by the fact that vowel sounds were not written down in Egyptian. Any written group of consonants could have been pronounced using one or more vowel sounds before, between or after, the letters forming the group. For instance, the word for 'sky' is written in Egyptian using the hieroglyphs for the consonants *p* and *t*. Are they pronounced 'epet', 'opet', 'pot', 'pat', 'peet', 'puat', 'peti', 'pata' etc. etc.? In other words, where do the vowels go! We shall see later how this problem of pronunciation can partially be solved.

The civilisation of Ancient Egypt lasted for over 3,000 years. It is to be expected that over such a period of time many changes in the grammar, vocabulary and pronunciation of the language would occur. The Egyptians were an intensely conservative people; hence their language and customs changed very slowly. But change they did. On several occasions, the changes were given an impetus by outside influences. For instance, in the fourteenth-century B.C., Egypt established an empire for herself in the Near East. One of the results of this was an influx of Near Eastern customs and ideas into Egypt; and a variety of non-Egyptian words was introduced into the Egyptian language.

Any language is bound to change as the centuries go by. Modern English, for example, is different from, say, the Victorian English of Dickens, a fact that was made amply clear a few years ago when volcanic eruptions forced the inhabitants of the island of Tristan da Cunha to seek refuge in Britain for a time. Islanders had been largely out of contact with the outside world since the nineteenth-century. On arrival in Britain the descendants of the original Victorian settlers were heard to speak in the Cockney used by Sam Weller; their vocabulary included many Victorian words and usages which have disappeared from English.

Victorian English was, in turn, different from that of Elisabethan times, exemplified by Shakespeare. And the fourteenth-century English of Chaucer, spoken less than 600 years ago, is almost like a foreign language to us. Take, for example, the first lines of the Prologue to his 'Canterbury Tales':

> 'When that Aprille with his shoures sote
> The Droghte of Marche hath perced to the rote,
> And bathed every veyne in swich licour,
> Of which vertu engendred is the flour . . .
> Than longen folk to goon on pilgrimages.'

Since Chaucer's time, the words he used have changed their meaning, ceased to be used, changed their spelling, as spoken English has evolved to what it is today. So, too, did Egyptian evolve. Spoken Egyptian, like English, had regional dialects. Very little written Egyptian reflects this, at least until the Christian era; official written Egyptian should probably be compared to standard 'B.B.C.' English.

The spoken language of Egypt changed more rapidly than the written. At times, they were in step; at other times, the written language lagged behind the spoken until an attempt was made to bridge the gap. At all times, monumental records on stone were more conservative than business documents or letters written on papyrus. The same sort of difference can be noted in English, where a letter written to, say, a friend, is couched in very different English from that used in, for instance, the law courts, which have a tendency to employ an English that uses archaic, legalistic terms.

Egyptologists have been able to discern four main stages in the development of the Egyptian language:

1. *Old Egyptian*: the language used from Dynasty I to Dynasty VI (*c.* 3100-2180 B.C.). Known mainly from religious texts inscribed in the pyramids of five kings of Dynasties V and VI (the Pyramid Texts) and from captions to the reliefs painted or sculpted on the walls inside *mastaba*-tombs, or from the biographies of the owners of these tombs engraved at the entrance of, or inside, the tomb.

2. *Middle Egyptian*: the language which came into use between Dynasty XI and Dynasty XII (2134-1786 B.C.). Regarded by Egyptian scribes as the classic stage of their language, it remained their ideal model until Roman times. Middle

Egyptian is a grammatically strict and balanced language in which, for a time, the written word was similar to the spoken. Written Middle Egyptian was used for religious texts, narratives, poetry, business and administrative documents. Eventually, however, its use was reserved for historical and religious inscriptions, on stone or papyrus. It was revived in the Graeco-Roman period and employed for temple inscriptions, where it was written in a cryptic and decorative script known as Ptolemaic.

3. *Late Egyptian* : the vernacular used from the end of Dynasty XVIII until Dynasty XXIV (1300-715 B.C.). Late Egyptian differs in syntax, grammar and vocabulary from Middle Egyptian, and the spoken language seems to have differed a great deal from the written. Evidence of this is found in letters, maxims and stories where colloquialisms, which were avoided in official documents, have crept in.

4. *Coptic* : the Egyptian language in its latest form, much changed from Old Egyptian. Used from third- to seventh-century A.D. when it was superseded by Arabic as the official language of the country, it is invaluable to the Egyptologist because, unlike Ancient Egyptian, its vowels are written down thus giving a clearer indication of how words were pronounced.

The Copts and Coptic

In 332 B.C. Alexander the Great conquered Egypt. From then on, until the Roman conquest in 30 B.C., Egypt was ruled by Greeks. The thirty-second and last dynasty of kings to rule Egypt before the coming of Christ was not Egyptian but Greek. The official language of the country during this period, the language spoken by the ruling classes and by educated persons, was Greek. The peasants spoke the same language as that spoken by their ancestors, although in a form which differed even more from the original Egyptian than modern English differs from Chaucer's. These descendants of the Ancient Egyptians are called 'Copts'; the language they spoke is called 'Coptic'.

The term 'Copt' comes from the Greek 'Aiguptos'—Egypt. This became *qibt* in Arabic, and Copt in English. Originally, the term Copt simply meant a native of Egypt; eventually, however, the term was reserved for reference to the Christian inhabitants of Egypt. This meaning of the word was first used in Europe in the sixteenth-century A.D.

For a long time, the Copts kept their language, which was spoken in several dialects. By A.D. 290, when Egypt became a Roman province and formed part of Rome's eastern empire, Christianity had spread throughout the Near East. The Christian Copts of Egypt wanted to write down the Bible, especially the Gospels, in their own language. However, their written language, consisting as it did of hieroglyphs, hieratic and demotic, was not well suited to this, the main disadvantage being the lack of written vowel sounds which would prevent an exact translation of Christian teachings being made.

The Copts solved the problem by adapting the Greek alphabet for their purposes by adding seven new signs to it to cover sounds not found in Greek. Thus Coptic is the latest form of the Ancient Egyptian language written not in hieroglyphs, hieratic or demotic but in Greek letters. Problems such as the one outlined above where the correct pronunciation of the word for sky, *pt*, was discussed, can be solved with the aid of Coptic. In Egyptian, 'sky' is written ⌐⌐ (the upper signs are uniliteral hieroglyphic signs, the lower sign is a determinative). In Coptic, this word is written   ⲧⲉ
From this we can deduce that the Egyptian consonants *p* and *t* should have the vowel 'e' placed between them in pronunciation, giving 'pet' as the spoken Egyptian for 'sky'.

The first 'Coptic' writings appeared around the third-century A.D. Over the next two centuries, a greater use of Coptic writing coincided with the growth of the Egyptian Christian church, the development of monasteries, the disappearance of hieroglyphs, the decline of Greek influence in Egypt combined with an upsurge of Egyptian, and therefore Coptic, nationalism.

The most original documents were the work of men such as St Anthony and St Pachom. Anthony, who was born *c.* A.D. 251, and Pachom, who was born *c.* A.D. 292, were the founders of the monastic system as it is known today. Their writings were mostly epistles, biographies of the Saints, and rules for their monasteries.

The most nationalistic of the Coptic monks was Shenute, who was born in A.D. 334. He took over from his uncle, Bgoul, as Head of the White Monastery at Sohag when he was fifty-one years old. By this time, Coptic art and architecture had broken away from the Pharaonic style. A new, Coptic, style was created, much influenced by Byzantine and Romanesque forms. At Sohag, however, Shenute built a church which looks very like an Ancient Egyptian temple. Shenute died in A.D. 452, at the age of 118 years ; he left behind a considerable amount of written work.

The year before Shenute died, in A.D. 451, the Council of Ephesus had been held. The result of the Council was the adoption by the Coptic Church of the Monophysite heresy —the belief that Christ had one nature, and that nature was divine not human. The Coptic Church broke away from the rest of Christendom.

After the Arab Conquest in A.D. 640, the Copts were decimated. Many converted to Islam ; their churches and monasteries were abandoned ; in the tenth-century, the last great Coptic scriptoria were closed. Eventually, most of Egypt was Arabic-speaking and Muslim. Enclaves of Christian Egyptians, the Copts, remained. They also spoke Arabic in everyday life ; but they continued to use Coptic in the liturgy of the Church, rather as Latin was used until recently in the Roman Catholic Church. The use of Coptic generally had died out by the sixteenth-century.

The Coptic language seems to have had five main dialects, each derived from the speech of a particular part of the country : (i) Fayûmic, used in the district around the Fayûm oasis ; (ii) Akhmimic, used in the region of the town of Akhmim in Upper Egypt ; (iii) Sub-Akhmimic, possibly used in the locality of Assiut ; (iv) Bohairic, possibly used in Memphis and the Delta ; and (v) Sahidic, used in the district of Thebes (modern-day Luxor) in Upper Egypt. Sahidic is the classical literary form of the language ; Bohairic is the dialect used in present-day Church liturgy.

Today, about one-tenth of the population of Egypt is Coptic. Few Copts can actually speak, write or understand Coptic ; their numbers are perhaps insufficient to ensure the survival for much longer of this last, tenuous, link with the language of Pharaonic Egypt.

The survival of Ancient Egyptian words in modern languages

In spite of the persistence of the Ancient Egyptian language through several millennia, and in spite of the influence Egypt had on her neighbours in the Near East, countries such as Nubia and the Sudan to the south, Syria and Palestine to the north-east (ruled by Egypt for centuries), and other countries adjacent to Syria-Palestine with whom Egypt maintained relations, warlike and otherwise; in spite of these things, the language of Ancient Egypt has left a surprisingly small mark on the languages of the world.

This might be expected in the cases of Nubia and the Sudan, or of Libya, because the native languages of these countries had no written record and were superseded by the languages of the invaders who came after the Egyptians. It is, however, more surprising in the countries to the east of Egypt. The Semites of these regions have left written records almost as old as the Egyptian ones; in the case of Mesopotamia, even older.

We know from the story of a famous Egyptian traveller, Wenamun, that around 1085 B.C. he met a man from as far away as Cyprus who could speak Egyptian. And yet, scarcely a hundred years later, when the oldest parts of the Bible were being written, very few Egyptian words were remembered.

Of the rich and varied Egyptian vocabulary of over 20,000 words, only five are found for certain in the Bible. Two of these words are measures of capacity: *ephah* from the Egyptian *ỉpt* (eighteen litres) and *hin* from the Egyptian *hnw* (a jar). The word *Pharaoh* comes from the Greek, pharao, which in turn comes from the Hebrew, par'o. In Egyptian, the term is *pr '3* (pronounced per aar) which means 'the Great House', a way of referring to the king by identifying him with the Royal Palace. Although we now tend to call the kings of Egypt 'Pharaohs', the Egyptians themselves did not always do so. Until Dynasty XVIII, the term *pr '3* simply referred to the palace; the earliest known example of the term being used to describe the king himself is found in a letter written to Akhenaten (Amenophis IV), the husband of the famous Nefertiti, in about 1360 B.C.

Two personal names found in the Bible are Egyptian in origin: *šsn*—lotus—became *shushan* (lily) in Hebrew, then the name Shushanna, which became Sousanna in Greek and Susanna(h) to us. *Petepre* (He-whom-Re-has-given) in Egyptian became

Potiphar in the Bible. The most famous Biblical character to have connections with Egypt is Moses. Egyptian had a word *msw* which means 'born'; however, there is some doubt as to whether this can be Moses, since in Hebrew Moses is written with a different s from that in *msw*.

Several Egyptian words have come down to us via the Greek: the Egyptian *hbny* was a tree which grew in Nubia and had hard, black wood. In Greek, *hbny* became *ebenos*, which in turn became our *ebony*. In Egyptian, *ḳmyt* was the juice from the acacia tree. *Kmyt* became *kommi* in Greek, *gummi* in Latin, *gum* in English. In Egyptian, the word *s3k* meant a receptacle or holder of some sort. In Greek, the word became *sakkos*, in Latin, *saccus*, in English, *sack*.

The worlds of geography, chemistry and geology owe some words to the Egyptians. The Greek word *oasis* is of Egyptian descent. The original word was *wḥ3t* (pronounced waa het), the literal meaning of which is 'cauldron'. The gas *ammonia* and the fossil *ammonite* are both derived from the name of one of Egypt's most powerful gods, Amun. There was a temple and an oracle of Amun at the Sîwa oasis in the western desert. The most famous person to consult the oracle of Amun was Alexander the Great; after Alexander, the Greeks and the Romans continued to honour Amun, whom they called Zeus Ammon and Jupiter Ammon respectively. *Sal ammoniacus* (ammoniac salt) was found near the temple at Sîwa, hence the term 'ammonia'. The animal that was sacred to Amun was a ram; Amun was often depicted wearing ram's horns. Hence, *ammonite* derives its name from its resemblance to these horns.

Our legacy of Ancient Egyptian words is small. Even the Eskimoes, whose language was written down less than 200 years ago, have given us words such as kayak, nunatak, igloo, anorak, almost as many as the Egyptians have given with their 3,000 years of hieroglyphic writing.

The final blow to Egyptian linguistic pride comes when one realises that even things which were peculiar to Egypt are not now referred to by their Egyptian names. What could be more Egyptian than pyramids, obelisks and mummies; or the famous Sphinx at Giza? Yet the words we use for these things are not Egyptian. In most cases, the words used demonstrate the truth of the saying 'the Greeks have a word for it'. In

Egyptian, the word for *pyramid* was *mr* ; our word 'pyramid' comes from the name of the little Greek cakes made of wheat and honey and shaped like pyramids—*puramides*. The Egyptian word for *obelisk* was *tẖn* ; the English word comes from the Greek *obeliskoi*— 'little spits'. The Greeks did not have a word for *mummy*. The Egyptian word was *wỉ*. The Arabic word for the gum or bitumen which was used for mummification purposes in the Late Period is *mumiya* ; hence the term 'mummy'.

As for the *Sphinx*. The word 'sphinx' is Greek; and the story of Oedipus shows that the Greeks themselves had a sphinx which took the shape of a winged lioness with a woman's head. This sphinx had a cruel nature and asked for answers to riddles on pain of death. The now-famous saying 'the riddle of the sphinx' refers to the riddle this sphinx asked, which was:

'What goes on four feet, on two feet, and three,
But the more feet it goes on the weaker it be ?'

to which Oedipus gave the answer that it was a man, who in infancy crawls upon all fours, in manhood goes upright on two feet, in old age needs the support of a staff. Upon hearing this answer, the sphinx killed herself.

The Egyptians had many sphinxes. They were normally divine lions with the head of a king. Occasionally, they were sphinxes of queens, with a queen's head upon the body of a lioness. Sometimes they took the form of a panther with a falcon's head, in order to protect the king and Egypt from enemies. Sometimes the sphinxes were surmounted by the head of an animal particularly connected with a certain god. This is the case at Karnak where there is a double row of sphinxes leading up to the main gateway of the Temple of Amun. Each of these sphinxes has the head of the ram which was sacred to Amun.

Unlike the Greek sphinx, Egyptian sphinxes were not cruel. They were a manifestation of divinity and royalty; their job was to protect tombs and temples, and to overcome enemies.

The most renowned, the largest and oldest of Egyptian sphinxes is the one at Giza, which is over 240' long and 65' high. It was carved out of a limestone knoll in front of the second largest pyramid in Dynasty IV, some 4,500 years ago. Its face is the face of

Chephren, whose pyramid at Giza is one of the trio which together formed one of the seven wonders of the ancient world. In the New Kingdom, the Sphinx of Giza was identified with a form of the sun god, and called 'Harmachis' (Horus-on-the-horizon). But even this most famous of sphinxes is known to us by a Greek and not an Egyptian word.

Even the words for the river *Nile* and for *Egypt* herself are not Egyptian. The Greeks called Egypt's great river by the general Semitic term for river, *nahal*, instead of by the Egyptian term, *ḥ'py*. The most popular name for Egypt as used by the Egyptians themselves was *kmt* or *keme* (the Black Land, a reference to the alluvial soil deposited by the annual Nile inundation). This became *al kimia* in Arabic, then *alchemy* and *chemistry* in English. The English words arose out of a confusion between the Arabic name for Egypt and the science which Europeans credited the Arabs with inventing—alchemy. Our word, *Egypt*, is derived from the Greek, *Aiguptos*. This in turn came from the Egyptian, *ḥwt-k3-Ptḥ*—Mansion of the Ka (or soul) of Ptah—a name of the old capital city of Egypt. The Greeks named the whole country after what they considered to be its chief city, a city to which they gave a Greek name, Memphis.

The modern world owes a debt to Ancient Egypt not for the legacy of words from the Egyptian language but for the fact that it was an Egyptian invention, papyrus, which enabled the great works of Greek and Roman literature to be transmitted and preserved and eventually to be inherited by us.

PART II

Grammar, exercises and vocabularies

This section of 'Introducing Egyptian hieroglyphs' aims to supply the reader with enough basic grammar and vocabulary for him to be able to attempt translations of simple Middle Egyptian texts and inscriptions.

It is arranged in eleven Lessons, at the end of each of which is a Vocabulary and a set of Exercises for the student to practise what he has learned in the preceding Lesson.

A Key to the Exercises will be found at the back of the book; so, also, will a glossary of all the words used in the Exercises. This is arranged under two headings—an Egyptian-English Vocabulary and an English-Egyptian Vocabulary.

A sign-list of the hieroglyphic signs used in Part II appears on pages 125-136.

LESSON 1

Direction of hieroglyphic writing

Hieroglyphic writing is a decorative script; scribes were at great pains to arrange the signs in an artistic way with no unsightly gaps or ugly groupings.

Inscriptions were written either in horizontal lines or in vertical columns (from top to bottom). In both cases the lines and the columns, and the individual signs within them, could be written either from right to left or from left to right. It has become the custom for modern printed books to adapt all hieroglyphic inscriptions so that when printed they are read from left to right, even though the original inscription may be read otherwise. This is done in order to simplify the reading of hieroglyphs when they accompany a western language.

The different directions in which hieroglyphs can be written are especially noticeable in inscriptions carved in stone where a decorative effect was being sought. For instance, inscriptions written around doorways can reflect the Egyptians' love of symmetry. Often, the same inscription is written on each side of an entrance. In order to keep a balance, the hieroglyphs on the left-hand side are written so that they face the door-way, and those on the right-hand side do likewise. The inscriptions above the doorway are divided into two halves, both equal in length and identical to look at, except that the signs on the right-hand side of the centre-point are read from left to right, and those on the left-hand side are read from right to left.

When reading a hieroglyphic inscription, the reader has first to decide the sequence in which the signs are to be read. There is an easy way to do this: observe the direction in which the signs depicting living things (human or animal) are facing. In nearly all cases, they will face the beginning of the inscription. The reader should therefore read *towards the faces* of living things. For example, the words 𓅱𓈖𓆓𓀀 must be read from left to right because the snake, the bird and the man all face towards the left.

E

In lines of hieroglyphs, and in the signs within the lines, upper has precedence over lower. For example, in the word ⟨glyphs⟩ the order of signs is ⟨glyph⟩ + ⟨glyph⟩ + ⟨glyph⟩ + ⟨glyph⟩ + ⟨glyph⟩ , + ⟨glyph⟩

The following examples illustrate the four possible ways of reading hieroglyphs. In each case, the arrows show the direction in which the writing is to be read; the letters give the order of the lines; and the numbers indicate the sequence of the individual signs.

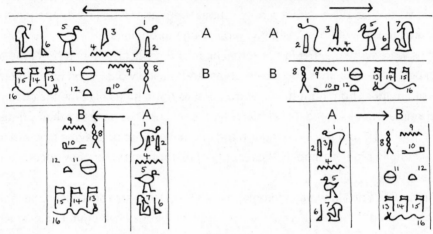

Note that the hieroglyphs are not divided into individual words; and that no punctuation signs are used.

Pronunciation

The Ancient Egyptian language, in common with Semitic languages such as Hebrew and Arabic, did not express its vowel sounds in written form. The reason for this is easy to find. It is a characteristic of the Semitic family of languages that words are pronounced differently according to grammatical use or context. For instance, the Egyptian word for house ⟨glyph⟩ may have been pronounced 'par' when used in isolation, 'per' when followed by a genitive, 'epraru' when used in the plural. In languages where vowels are changed to indicate the uses of words, it is easy to assume that consonants are all that matter; hence, in the written language, vowels are not indicated.

In Egyptian, the word for sky is written 𓊪𓏏𓇯 . We know that 𓊪 is *p* and 𓏏 is *t*. The 𓇯 is a sign which indicates the meaning of the first two signs. It is called a determinative and is not pronounced. Egyptian has many of these signs (see page 66). *p* and *t* are two consonants. In general, consonants by themselves are not pronounceable. The problem of pronouncing several of them strung together to make a word has been solved by Egyptologists by the expedient of inserting an 'e' wherever there seems to be a need for a vowel. Hence, the *p* and *t* of the word 'sky' are usually pronounced 'pet'.

In this instance, the pronunciation is probably close to the way in which the Ancient Egyptians pronounced the word. We know that in Coptic, the word for sky is ⲡⲉ , pronounced 'pay'. It can be deduced from this that the Middle Egyptian word *pt* was pronounced 'pet'. The final letter of the word, *t*, had fallen away by the time the word had reached the Coptic period. This is because, like the English letter g, the Egyptian letter *t* is weak. In both languages, weak letters placed at the ends of words tend to fall away. For example, in English, getting can become gettin'; going become goin'.

Transliteration

When translating Egyptian texts, the beginner will find it useful to *transliterate* them before attempting a *translation*. Transliteration in this instance means turning the hieroglyphic signs into an approximation of English alphabetic signs. Thus, the sentence used above in our example of writing direction is *transliterated* and *translated* as follows:

Transliteration   ḏd mdw ỉn Gb ḥn' psḏt.f
Translation   For recitation by Geb and his Ennead
                          (see Vocabulary 1 below)

Introducing Egyptian Hieroglyphs

The alphabet

The Egyptians never adopted an entirely alphabetic system of writing. They did, however, have an alphabet, consisting of twenty-four letters, which they used with their many other signs, their phonograms and ideograms. The letters of the Egyptian alphabet are listed below. At first glance some of the letters in transliteration look similar to some of the vowels used in English. It should be remembered, however, that Ancient Egyptian had no written vowels.

The alphabet

Sign	Transliteration	Object depicted	Approximate pronunciation
🦅	3	vulture	a as in father
𓇋	ỉ	flowering reed	i as in filled
𓇋𓇋 (or \\ )	y	two reeds	y as in discovery
⌐	'	arm & hand	a as in car
🐦	w	quail chick	oo as in too also w as in wet
𓃀	b	foot	b as in boot

Sign	Transliteration	Object depicted	Approximate pronunciation
▢	p	stool	p as in pedestal
✗〜	f	horned viper	f as in feel
🦉	m	owl	m as in moon
〜〜〜	n	water	n as in noon
⬯	r	mouth	r as in right
⌐⊔	h	reed shelter	h as in hat
𓎛	ḥ	wick of twisted flax	h as in ha!
⊘	ẖ	placenta (?)	ch as in loch
🐟	ḫ	animal's belly with teats	ch as in German ich
(i) ⌡ (ii) ─╫─	s	(i) folded cloth (ii) door bolt	s as in saw
⬭	š	pool	sh as in show

Sign	*Transliteration*	*Object depicted*	*Approximate pronunciation*
𓈎	ḳ	hill-slope	like q in queen
𓎡	k	basket with handle	k as in basket
𓎼	g	jar stand	g as in go
𓏏	t	loaf	t as in tap
𓍿	ṯ	tethering rope	like ch in church
𓂧	d	hand	d as in dog
𓆓	ḏ	snake	dj as in adjust

Notes on the alphabet

Since we do not know how the Egyptians named the letters of their alphabet, the hieroglyps 𓄿 *3*, 𓇋 *ỉ* and 𓂝 ’ have been given Hebrew names. *3* is ’aleph, *ỉ* is yodh and ’ is ’ayin.

The aleph, 𓄿, although pronounced like the a in father, is not a vowel but a weak consonant.

The yodh, 𓇋, should not be confused with the English i; although at first glance the yodh looks like a lower case English i, careful inspection of the transliteration of the sign will show that the dot on the i has been replaced by a ᵓ .

The hieroglyphs 𓇋 *ỉ* and 𓅱 *w* are consonants which bear a close resemblance to the English vowels i and u; hence they are known as semi-vowels.

Vocabulary to Lesson 1

ḏd mdw (djed medoo) for recitation

ỉn (inn) by

Gb (geb) Geb, the earth god

nb (neb) every, any, all (cf. Lesson 4)

ḥn' (hena) together with

psḏt (pes-jet) Ennead or group of 9 gods

pt (pet) sky, heaven

sḥtp (sehetep) to pacify

pr (per) house

nỉwt (newt) town, city

sḥr (secher) plan, counsel

ḥt (chet) thing

pn (pen) this m(asculine) follows its noun (cf. Lesson 4)

tn (ten) this f(eminine) follows its noun (cf. Lesson 4)

ky (key) other, another m. precedes its noun (cf. Lesson 4)

kt (ket) other, another f. precedes its noun (cf. Lesson 4)

EXERCISE 1

1. Learn and write out from memory the letters of the Egyptian alphabet.

2. Learn and write out from memory the words in Vocabulary 1.

   N.B. The above exercises should be written in both hieroglyphs and transliteration. The transliteration will help the beginner to memorise the hieroglyphs. Now, and at all stages, the hieroglyphs should be written with care, and the motto 'practice makes perfect' borne in mind ! The best results in writing hieroglyphs can be obtained if a drawing pen such as the Rotring 'Rapidograph', size 0.3, is used.

3. Write in hieroglyphs the following combinations of letters:

    3tp, i̯33t, 't, wbn, ptpt, md̲t, nbyt, rwd

    Try to group the letters in the way that an Egyptian scribe might have done, with no ugly gaps between them.

LESSON 2

Ideograms and phonograms

There were two classes of signs in Egyptian hieroglyphic writing: ideograms and phonograms.

Ideograms are sense-signs; that is, they represent either the object depicted or some closely related idea. For instance, ⊙ not only means 'sun' but also 'day' or 'daytime' or 'daylight'. When the ideogram stands for the actual object depicted, it is usually followed by a stroke: e.g. r 'sun'; $ḥr$ 'face'.

Phonograms are sound-signs; that is, they give the sound value associated with a sign. The sign may originally have been an ideogram; eventually it ceased to be used solely to denote an object and, by the rebus principle explained on page 37 came to represent objects or ideas which chanced to have a sound similar to that of the original sign. For example, the ideogram ⌣ means 'mouth' and is transliterated r. r is also the preposition meaning 'towards' and can therefore be written by what is now the phonogram ⌣.

There are three kinds of phonogram:

1. Those which represent single consonants and are called *uniliteral* signs e.g. the signs of the alphabet.
2. Those which represent a combination of two consonants and are called *biliteral* signs e.g. $\underline{\underline{\hphantom{x}}} = m + n$ (usually written *mn*);
   $\square = p + r$ (*pr*).
3. Those which represent a combination of three consonants and are called *triliteral* signs e.g. $= n + f + r$ (*nfr*);
   $= ḥ + t + p$ (*ḥtp*).

Biliteral and triliteral signs were used in much the same way as symbols such as & @ % £ are used in modern languages, that is, they are a convenient way of enlarging the alphabet by means of shorthand.

Phonetic complements

Sometimes a biliteral or triliteral sign has two or more sound values. The Egyptians introduced the system of *phonetic complements* in order to indicate which sound was to be read. For example, the triliteral sign ⌂ *ḥtp* was made easier to read by the addition of the two uniliteral signs ⌂ ▢ (*t*+*p*), giving the group ⌂▢. The reading of this group is still *ḥtp* (not *ḥtptp*) ; the last two signs are there simply to help the reader decide on the way in which the sign ⌂ is to be read. Similarly, the biliteral sign ⌷ is read *mn* ; in texts it is usually written ⌷. However, it is still read *mn* (not *mnn*) ; the final *n* confirms that the reading of the biliteral sign is *mn*.

At the beginning of each of the following lessons, examples of biliteral and triliteral signs will be given. If possible, they should be learned.

Determinatives

The Egyptian scribes were faced with the problem of making clear the exact meaning of their written words. All languages have words which are homophones, that is, words which sound the same but have different meanings—the words 'wear' and 'were' ; 'flour' and 'flower' in English, for example. The problem was made more difficult in Egyptian because the vowel sounds were not written. Thus, although many words may have been pronounced differently when spoken, they have the same appearance as each other when written. The confusion this could lead to will be appreciated if the following English words are read *ignoring the vowels* : leap, lop, alp, elope, lip, lap ; slope, slip, slap, sleep, asleep ; flop, flip, flap. It can be seen that a string of consonants can be very much modified as to reading and meaning by the addition of one or more vowels!

The Egyptians solved the problem by using ideograms. For example, 𓈎𓋴 *ḥs* can mean 'to freeze' or 'to turn back'. In the spoken language, the word may have been pronounced differently according to meaning; in the written language, the only way the Egyptians had of distinguishing one meaning from the other was by using an ideogram (an idea-o-gram) at the end of the word to make the meaning clear. Thus, the ideogram 𓊝 (a sail) placed after *ḥs* gives 𓈎𓋴𓊝, which means 'to freeze', the sail being used to indicate a (cold) wind. The ideogram 𓂻 (walking legs) placed after *ḥs* gives 𓈎𓋴𓂻, which means 'turn back'.

When used in this way, ideograms are called '*determinatives*' because they determine the meaning of the signs written before them. For example, the word 𓇜 *šsp* has at least four meanings; by using determinatives, the scribe could differentiate between them:

𓇜𓀜 = *šsp* 'accept'

𓇜⌒ = *šsp* 'palm' (a unit of length)

𓇜𓀾 = *šsp* 'statue'

𓇜𓁶 = *šsp* 'daylight'.

Determinatives are used with almost every word. A word indicating that someone is walking, running, marching is often followed by the determinative 𓂻 , which is a sign representing legs. In order to illustrate an intangible idea, a product of the mind, the sign 𓏛 , which represents a rolled-up papyrus, is used. Thus determinatives can be used with abstract ideas as well as concrete objects.

Ideograms which act as determinatives to a number of different words cannot express the specific meaning of those words, but only the *kind* of sense borne by them. They are therefore called *generic determinatives*.

Determinatives were added to phonetic signs to indicate what the word represented. They have a *visual* value only; they are *not pronounced*.

Determinatives also serve another useful purpose. There were no gaps between words in written Egyptian, the signs followed on from each other in one unbroken sequence. Since determinatives only came at the ends of words, they can serve to aid the reader in breaking up the hieroglyphic signs into separate words.

There were over 100 generic determinatives in Egyptian; here is a list of some of the more important, which should be studied carefully so that the meanings indicated by the signs become familiar:

Hieroglyph	*Illustrates*	*Used as determinative to indicate*
	seated man	men, men's names
	man with hand to mouth	eat, drink, speak, think
	man with basket on head	carry, lift, load
	man with sword	enemy, death
	man with stick	strength, action
	man with arms raised	praise, adore, greet
	young child	child, youth

Hieroglyph	Illustrates	Used as determinative to indicate
	seated woman	women, women's names
	seated man and woman	people
	seated god (note straight wig, curved beard)	god, king
	seated king (note coif, straight beard, uraeus on brow)	king
	king with flagellum	king
	king on stool	revered person, dead
	man leaning on staff	old, lean upon
	man with staff	official
	eye	see, sight
	ear of ox?	ear, hear
	nose, eye and cheek	nose, breath, joy

Hieroglyph	Illustrates	Used as determinative to indicate
	arms embracing	embrace, hold
	legs walking	go, come, enter
	legs walking backwards	retreat, withdraw
	leg	movement
	bull	cattle
	cow's skin	skin, animal
	piece of flesh	limbs, flesh
	pintail duck flying	fly
	swallow (note swallow tail)	great
	sparrow (note rounded tail)	bad, small
	cobra	goddess, especially those who took the form of cobra, e.g. Edjo, the Uraeus Goddess of Lower Egypt

Hieroglyph	Illustrates	Used as determinative to indicate
	herb	plant, flower
	branch	tree, wood
	sky	sky, heaven, above
	sun	sun, light, time
	sunshine	rays, shine
	sky with star suspended from it	night, dark
	flaming brazier	fire, heat, cook
	three ripples of water	water
	tongue of land	land, field, earth, river bank
	road bordered by shrubs	road, travel
	hill country	desert, foreign land

Hieroglyph	Illustrates	Used as determinative to indicate
⟍	throw-stick	foreign, foreigner
⌷	house	house, building
⌣⌐⌂	boat on water	boat, navigate, sail north (Nile flows south to north), downstream, with flow of river
⛵	ship under sail	sail south, upstream, against flow of river therefore sail used
⚑	cloth on pole, emblem of divinity	god
▽∘	knife	knife, cut
⌵	hoe	cultivate, hack up
✕	two sticks crossed	break, divide, reckon
⚱	beer jug	pot, vessel, anoint, liquid

A comprehensive list of hieroglyphic signs can be found in Gardiner's 'Egyptian Grammar', pp. 438-548.

Vocabulary to Lesson 2

⊙ᛁ *r'* (ray) sun

ḥr (her) face

r (ro) mouth

ḥs (hes) to freeze ; with determinative ⌒ , to turn back (*ḥsỉ*)

ššp (shesep) to accept, receive

palm

statue

daylight

nfr (nefer) good, beautiful, happy (cf. Lesson 4)

t (tar) bread (also written ⊖)

ḥnḳt (henket) beer (also written ⊖)

rnpt (renpet) year

drt (deret) hand (varr. *ḏrt* (djeret))

mnt (ment) thigh

spt (sepet) lip

ḥf3w (hefaroo) snake

EXERCISE 2

1. Practise writing hieroglyphs by writing out the determinatives from the list given above.

2. Write in hieroglyphs the following combinations of letters, remembering to take care to group them according to Egyptian usage !
   h3w, h3t, ḥb, ḫt, ẖt, sbḳ, šbw, ḳbḥ, k3, gr, tỉtỉ, twt, ṯsm, dn, ḏt

F

LESSON 3

Some common biliteral signs

3w		3b, mr		3ḫ		ỉw	
ỉm, gs		ỉm		ỉn		ỉr	
ỉs		ʾ3		ʿḳ		ʿḏ	

Some common triliteral signs

ỉwn		ʿwt		ʿnḫ		ʿḥ3		ʿḥʿ	

Nouns

In English, a noun is the *name* of something. For example, in the sentence 'the teacher sent the naughty girl to be punished by the headmaster', the words 'teacher', 'girl' and 'headmaster' are *nouns*. The words 'angry' and 'naughty' are *adjectives*, that is, they are words which *describe* a noun.

In English, adjectives do not change their form; 'naughty' would still be written in the same way if it had been used to describe a boy and not a girl, or if it had been used to describe several girls. In many languages, however, adjectives do change their form, according to the *gender* of the noun they are describing. If an adjective is being used to describe a masculine noun it is written in a different way from one used to describe a feminine noun. In both cases it is possible to find a third way of writing the adjective if it is being used to describe a plural noun.

Gender

Egyptian nouns have two genders, *feminine* and *masculine*. Most feminine nouns end in *t* e.g. ☖⳿ *st* 'woman', ⌾ *nîwt* 'town'. Nouns which do not end in *t* are usually masculine e.g. ⌾ *r* 'sun', ⌾ *ḥr* 'face'. The sense of the English *neuter* (it, thing) is expressed in Egyptian by the feminine e.g. ⌾ *dwt* 'evil thing'.

Definite and indefinite article

In Middle Egyptian the article, whether definite (the) or indefinite (a, an) is not normally written. Thus, ⌾ *rn* may be translated as 'the name', 'a name' or 'name' according to context.

Writing the plural

In English, nouns denoting one thing are *singular*, whilst those denoting more than one thing are *plural*. The plural is usually formed simply by adding an s to the singular, as: book, books; or by changing the last letter(s) of the noun before adding an s, as: fly, flies; wife, wives. Some nouns change completely from singular to plural, as: man, men; foot, feet.

There are two ways of indicating the plural in Egyptian:

1. the singular form can be written out three times:

   e.g. *singular*   *plural*

   ⌷ *pr* 'house'   ⌷ *prw* 'houses'

   ⌾ *rn* 'name'   ⌾ *rnw* 'names'

   Note that in transliteration a *w* added to the end of the word indicates plural.

2. a determinative consisting of three strokes which can be written ⁝⁝⁝ ; ⁝'⁝' or ,⁝
according to artistic preference, can be used:

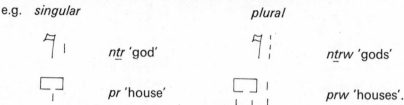

e.g.   *singular*   *plural*

ntr 'god'   *ntrw* 'gods'

pr 'house'   *prw* 'houses'.

The dual form

If the Egyptian scribe wished to indicate *pairs* of things or persons he used what we call
the *dual form* which is indicated by writing out the singular noun twice instead of three
times as in the plural. Sometimes, the sign   is used to indicate the dual; in this case,
the   is added to the singular form of the noun and the determinative is written twice.
This second method is most often used with words which are commonly written with
several hieroglyphic signs:

e.g.   *singular*   *dual*

pr 'house'   *prwy* 'two houses'

irt 'eye'   *irty* 'two eyes'

ntr 'god'   *ntrwy* 'pair of gods'

snt 'sister'   *snty* 'two sisters'

Transliteration of plural and dual forms

It will be noted from the examples above that in *transliteration* the *masculine plural* is
rendered by adding a -*w* onto the singular noun e.g. *pr* 'house' has the plural *prw*
'houses'. The *masculine dual* is -*wy* e.g. *ntr* 'god' has the dual *ntrwy*; the *feminine dual*
is -*y* e.g. *snt* 'sister' has the dual *snty*.

It has already been pointed out that the *singular feminine* ending is *t* e.g. 🔥 *st*

'woman'. In transliteration, the *plural feminine* ending is -wt e.g. ⌐⌐𝕊| swt 'women'.
The Egyptian scribe often omitted to write out plural and dual endings.

Numbers

The writing of numerals
A vertical stroke | is used when writing the numbers 1-9; special signs are used to
write the multiples of ten. The seven signs employed are:

1	|	(w')	10,000	ſ	(db')
10	∩	(md)	100,000	𓆓	(hfn)
100	𐎨	(št)	1,000,000	𓁀	(hh)

1,000 𓆼 (h3)

The higher values are written in front of the lower. If an Egyptian scribe wished to write
the number 1,245, he would start with the highest value sign (𓆼 —1,000) then the
next highest (𐎨 —100, writing the sign twice to indicate 200); then the tens and the
units, each being written out as many times as necessary to indicate the total—four
times in the case of the tens, five for the units; thus he would write 1,245 as 𓆼𐎨𐎨∩∩∩∩||||.

e.g. 𓆼𐎨𐎨||| ||| 1,208

𐎨𐎨𐎨∩∩'''
𐎨𐎨 ∩∩''' 546

ſſſ ∩∩∩ 30,030

Cardinal numbers

1. The numeral *follows* the noun; the noun is usually in the singular form:

e.g.   ⲧⲛ ‖   *s* 2   '2 men'

      ⲙⲏ ∩   *mḥ* 10   '10 cubits'.

2. The words for 1,000 and 1,000,000 are sometimes written *before* their noun, which is written in the singular, and are connected to it by 𓅓 *m* (being) or 〰 *n* (of):

    e.g. 𓆼𓅓𓏏 *ḫ3 m t ḥnḳt* 'a thousand of bread and beer' (lit: a thousand being bread and beer)

      𓆼〰𓏦 *ḫ3 n rnpwt* 'a thousand years' (lit: a thousand of years).

Vocabulary to Lesson 3

𓊨𓁐 *st* woman

𓇳 *r'* sun

� *ḏwt* evil, sadness

〰 *rn* name

𓊹 *nṯr* god

𓁹 *îrt* eye

𓊃𓈖𓏏𓁐 *snt* sister

𓊨𓏤 *s* man

𓐝 *mḥ* cubit

𓅱𓏏 *w3t* way, road, side

𓊞 *ds* jug

�dmi *dmî* town

var. 𓎟 *nb* lord, master

varr. 𓇾 , 𓇾 *t3* earth, land

𓇾𓇾 *t3wy* the Two Lands i.e. Egypt

var. 𓇓𓅱 *nsw* king, king of Upper Egypt

var. 𓆎𓏏𓊖 *Kmt* the Black Land i.e. Egypt

var. *nḥḥ* eternity

varr. 𓅨 , 𓁷 *wr* prince, great one

ḥmt woman, wife

s3t daughter

šrr small

later *šrî* small

EXERCISE 3

(a) *Write in hieroglyphs and transliteration*

    1. two hands   2. two thighs   3. two lips

    4. twenty years   5. seventy-five snakes   6. a thousand towns.

Lesson 3   79

(b) *Translate into English*

1. 𓅱𓃭𓏏 𓏭

2. 𓄿𓄿𓄿 𓎡𓎡𓎡 𓏭𓏭𓏭 〰 𓆑 𓂋

3. 𓆑 𓂝 𓎡𓎡𓎡

4. 𓊗 𓏏

5. 𓋴𓊪𓏏𓆄𓊪𓂋

LESSON 4

More biliteral signs

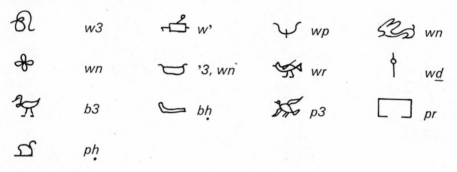

	w3		*w'*		*wp*		*wn*
	wn		*'3, wn*		*wr*		*wd*
	b3		*bḥ*		*p3*		*pr*
	pḥ						

More triliteral signs

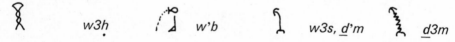

	w3ḥ		*w'b*		*w3s, d'm*		*d3m*

The genitive

In English, the genitive is expressed by the word 'of' e.g. 'the knave *of* hearts', 'the Queen *of* the May'.

There are two ways of expressing the genitive in Egyptian: one in which the 'of' is written, the other in which it is not. The former is called the *indirect genitive*, the latter is called the *direct genitive*.

1. *The direct genitive* is formed by placing two nouns next to each other with no intervening word, as if in English we were to express the phrase 'Lord of the Two

Lands' as 'Lord the Two Lands' e.g. ▽ 🗏 *nb t3wy* 'Lord (of) the Two Lands'. The direct genitive is used when the connection between the two nouns is particularly close, although this is not an absolute rule.

2. *The indirect genitive* uses the so-called *genitival adjective* ∿∿∿ *ny* by interposing it between the two nouns e.g. 'the King of Egypt' 𓆧 ∿∿ 𓅱 ∿∿ 🗏 𓊖 *nsw ny Kmt*.

The genitival adjective changes according to whether the noun which goes before it is masculine, feminine or plural.

   If the preceding noun is *masculine*, the genitive is written ∿∿∿ *ny*, as in 'the King of Egypt'—*nsw ny Kmt*—above.

   If the preceding noun is *feminine*, the genitive is written ∿∿∿ *nyt* e.g 𓊖 ∿∿∿ 𓏭𓏭𓇳 *niwt nyt nḥḥ* 'the city of eternity'.

   If the preceding noun is *plural*, the genitive is written 𓏥 *nyw* when the noun is masculine, or ∿∿∿ *nywt* when the noun is feminine e.g. 𓅱𓅱𓅱 𓅱𓏥 *wrw nyw niwt* 'the great ones of the city'; 𓄿 𓅱𓏥 ∿∿∿ 𓀀𓏥 *ḥmwt nywt wrw* 'the wives of the chiefs'.

The *transliterations* given above of the genitival adjective are somewhat pedantic. It is more usual to transliterate the masculine singular as *n*, not as *ny*; the feminine singular as *nt*, not *nyt*; and the plural, both masculine and feminine, as *nw*, not as *nyw* and *nywt*.

Generally speaking, the indirect genitive is more commonly used than the direct.

Adjectives

In Egyptian, adjectives *follow* the nouns which they are describing, and *agree with them in number and gender* (see pages 75-76 for writings of feminine and plural) :

e.g.   〔hieroglyphs〕 *sḫr pn bin* 'this evil counsel' (lit: counsel this evil)

〔hieroglyphs〕 *ḫt nbt nfrt* 'every good thing' (lit: thing every good)

〔hieroglyphs〕 *s3t šrit* 'the little daughter' (lit: daughter little)

An exception to the rule that adjectives follow their nouns is *ky* (m.), *kt* (f.) 'other', 'another', which *precedes* its noun:

e.g.   〔hieroglyphs〕 *ky rn* 'another name'

〔hieroglyphs〕 *kt ḫt* 'another thing'.

Adjectives can be used to form nouns. In this case they usually have an appropriate determinative.

e.g. 〔hieroglyphs〕 *šri* 'small boy' i.e. adjective 〔hieroglyphs〕 (small) plus the determinative 〔hieroglyph〕

〔hieroglyphs〕 *nfrt* 'beautiful woman' i.e. adjective 〔hieroglyphs〕 (beautiful) plus feminine ending 〔hieroglyph〕 plus determinative 〔hieroglyph〕

〔hieroglyphs〕 *nfrt* 'fine cow' i.e. adjective 〔hieroglyphs〕 plus feminine ending plus determinative 〔hieroglyph〕.

Vocabulary to Lesson 4

〔hieroglyphs〕 *ḥm* male servant

〔hieroglyphs〕 *ḥmt* female servant

〔hieroglyphs〕 var. 〔hieroglyphs〕 *ḥm* Majesty

〔hieroglyphs〕 *wbn* to shine

〔hieroglyphs〕 *hrw* day, daytime

〔hieroglyphs〕 *mnḫ* (be) efficient

〔hieroglyphs〕 *sḫty* fowler, peasant

〔hieroglyphs〕 varr. 〔hieroglyphs〕 , 〔hieroglyph〕 *imy-r* overseer

〔hieroglyphs〕 *inw* produce

〔hieroglyphs〕 *sḫt* country

〔hieroglyphs〕 *mw* water

〔hieroglyphs〕 *it* father

〔hieroglyphs〕 *b3kt* handmaiden

〔hieroglyphs〕 *ḥnwt* mistress

〔hieroglyphs〕 var. 〔hieroglyphs〕 *ḥm-nṯr* priest

EXERCISE 4

(a) *Write in hieroglyphs and transliteration*

1. This beautiful house.
2. This beautiful woman.
3. The wife of the priest.
4. The house of the master.
5. An efficient overseer of the city.

(b) *Translate into English*

1. [hieroglyphs]

2. [hieroglyphs]

3. [hieroglyphs]

4. [hieroglyphs]

5. [hieroglyphs]

LESSON 5

More biliteral signs

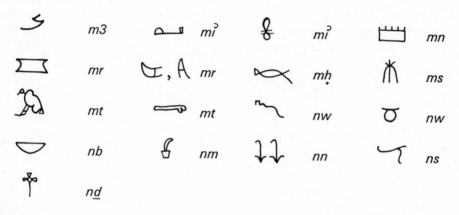

	m3		*mỉ*		*mỉ*		*mn*
	mr		*mr*		*mḥ*		*ms*
	mt		*mt*		*nw*		*nw*
	nb		*nm*		*nn*		*ns*
	nḏ						

More triliteral signs

	mwt		*nfr*		*nṯr*		*nḏm*		*wḥm*

Prepositions

In English, a *preposition* is a word which shows the relationship between a noun or pronoun and some other word in a sentence. For example, in the phrases 'the book is *in* my hand', 'the book is *beside* my hand', 'the book is *under* my hand', the words 'in', 'beside' and 'under' are all prepositions.

The chief prepositions in Egyptian are:

1.   𓅓 *m* (before suffix-pronouns (see page 92) written   𓇋𓅓 *im*) *in, from with*

   (i) 'in' a place e.g. in the house

   (ii) 'in' time e.g. in summer, for three years

   (iii) 'from' a place e.g. I went out from the house

   (iv) 'with' an instrument e.g. with my strong arm

2.   𓂋 *r to, towards; against*

   (i) 'to' a place e.g. to heaven, to the city, towards the house

   (ii) 'against' somebody e.g. I took action against my enemy

3.   𓈖 *n to* a person (i.e. the dative) e.g. I speak to the boy, I gave it to my mother

4.   𓁷 *ḥr upon, because* (𓁶 before suffix-pronouns)

   (i) 'upon' a place e.g. upon the water, on my feet

   (ii) cause e.g. pleased with (because of) something; on account of; sad concerning (because of) someone; about

5.   𓈖 *in by* e.g. for recitation by Geb

6.   𓐍𓆑𓏏 *ḫft in front of* e.g. before your face

7.   � *mỉ like* e.g. like a dream

8.   𓎛𓈖 *ḥn' together with* e.g. with his Ennead

9.   𓅓𓄤 *m-bȝḥ in the presence of, before* e.g. before the king

10.   𓅓𓆱 *m-ḫt after* e.g. after death, after he died

Adverbs

Adverbs are words whose main function is to describe verbs; they can also describe any part of speech except a noun or a pronoun. For example, in the following sentences: 'the boy came early'; 'the bird sang sweetly'; 'he works hard'; 'the river flows fast', the words early, sweetly, hard and fast are adverbs.

Sometimes, an adverb is expanded into a phrase, thus forming the so-called 'adverbial phrase'. For example, in the sentence 'we rise early', 'early' is an adverb describing the verb 'rise'. If 'early' were to be expanded into a phrase, it could become 'we rise *at six o'clock in the morning*'. Adverbial phrases can be made up of a preposition plus a noun e.g. 'the cows were sold *in the market*'. Further examples of adverbial phrases are 'they met him *on his arrival*'; 'he waited *until 4 o'clock*'.

Egyptian has very few true adverbs. It makes up for the lack by using *adverbial phrases* which are *formed by placing a preposition before a noun* (see English examples above).

e.g. the sun rises *in the sky* wbn r' m pt

he went *into the city on this day* pr.f r niwt m hrw pn

(the words *underlined* are adverbial phrases).

Vocabulary to Lesson 5

bw place

R' Re, the sun god

wr great (adj.)

grḥ night

hrw day

r-ḏrw to the limits of

ḫt body, belly

iwnn sanctuary

sḫnt four supports of heaven

ḏd to say, to tell

sḏm to hear, to obey

h3b to send

var. , rdi̯ or di̯ to give, to place

EXERCISE 5

(a) *Write in hieroglyphs and transliteration*
1. To another place.
2. To Geb, together with Re.
3. In this great name.
4. In all lands.
5. In the presence of Ptah.

(b) *Translate into English*

1.

2.

3.

4.

LESSON 6

One of the things that the reader will notice about Ancient Egyptian inscriptions, whether they be short or long, on the walls or columns of temples, on the walls of tombs, on the lids of coffins, on decorative bands on furniture, or on statue bases, is that in many of them one or more *cartouches* stand out.

We have already seen that Champollion used cartouches as the starting point from which he was able to decipher hieroglyphs. So, too, can the reader use them for his first attempts to read 'real' hieroglyphs as opposed to those in the Exercises he may have been attempting as he reads through this book.

From the latter part of the Old Kingdom onwards, each king of Egypt adopted a royal titulary on his accession to the throne; this titulary consisted of five names. From Dynasty V onwards, the last two were put inside cartouches when they were written in inscriptions. The cartouche names were: 'the King of Upper and Lower Egypt (⯑ *nsw bịt*) ⯑ ; 'the Son of Re (⯑ *s3 R'*) ⯑ . The former is the religious name of the king, adopted on his succession to the throne, the latter is the name borne by the king before his accession and is almost equivalent to a family name.

The most desirable way to practise reading cartouches is, of course, to go to Egypt and find them on the monuments there! As this is not practicable for everyone, a visit to the nearest museum, which will probably have at least some Egyptian objects in its collection, will have to suffice.

In order to help the reader when he first comes into contact with cartouches, the following examples are given for him to attempt to translate. All the words used in the following cartouches will be found in the Egyptian-English Vocabulary on page 137. As usual the answers will be found in the Key to Exercises.

EXERCISE 6

Hints before starting

Modern interpretations of the ways in which kings' names are transliterated, and pronounced, vary, due mainly to the lack of written vowels in Egyptian. Several versions
will be found in books of Egyptology; in fact, the form of royal name used is more
often than not the Greek rather than the Egyptian.

In cartouches where an element of the king's name is the name of a god, then the god's
name was written first out of reverence even though it might be pronounced last. e.g.
the name of the Dynasty IV king, Mycerinus, is written ⟨☉ ⚊ 𝗨𝗨𝗨⟩; *R'* (☉)
mn (⚊) *k3w* (𝗨 𝗨 𝗨) with the name of the sun god, Re, written first. It is,
however, read *mn-k3w-R'*—abiding (*mn*) are the spirits (*k3w*) of Re (*R'*). Mycerinus
is the Greek form of *mn-k3w-R'*.

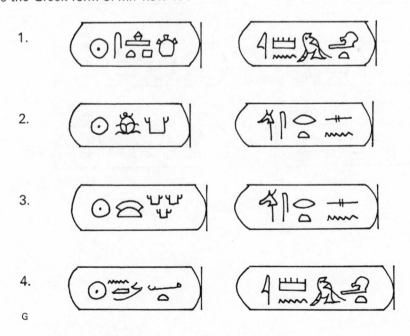

1.

2.

3.

4.

G

5.

6.

7.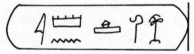

8.

9.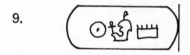

10.

LESSON 7

More biliteral signs

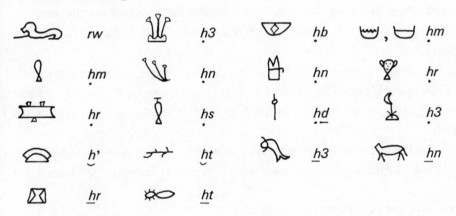

rw		ẖ3		ḥb		,	ḥm
ḥm		ḥn		ḥn			ḥr
ḥr		ḥs		ḥd			ḥ3
ḥ'		ẖt		ḫ3			ḫn
ḫr		ḫt					

More triliteral signs

rwḏ   ḥ3t   ḥk3   ḥtp   ḫpr

Pronouns

In English, a pronoun is a word that stands in place of a noun. Without pronouns, English sentences would be very clumsy. For instance:

'Robert went to the shelf. Robert picked up a book. Robert read the book. Then Robert gave the book to Robert's sister. Robert and Robert's sister liked the book when Robert and Robert's sister had read the book.'

When the above paragraph is rewritten using, where necessary, pronouns in place of nouns, a more satisfactory version is obtained:

'Robert went to the shelf and picked up a book. He read the book and then gave it to his sister. Both Robert and his sister liked the book when they had read it.'

The words underlined in the above paragraph are pronouns: he, it, his, they. They demonstrate between them three different ways of using pronouns:

(i) *He* read, *they* had read, are examples of pronouns indicating the persons *performing an action*. In other words, they are the *subjects* of the verb and of the sentence.

(ii) Gave *it*, had read *it*, are examples of pronouns which are *objects* of an action.

(iii) *His* sister is an example of a pronoun being used to show *possession*. In this case, the pronoun is acting like an adjective. It is, therefore, a possessive pronoun.

Egyptian has several classes of pronoun, each of which is put to different use or uses. Only two classes of pronoun will be dealt with here; as in English, they have three *persons*:

1st person, singular and plural: I, we, etc.
2nd person, singular and plural: thou, you, etc.
3rd person, singular and plural: he, she, it, they, etc.

1. *Suffix-pronouns*, so called because they must *follow* and *be joined on to* (suffixed to) a preceding word:

Singular		Plural
.*i̯* I, my, me	1st person m and f	.*n* we, our, us
.*k* thou, thy, thee .*t* thou. thy, thee	2nd person m f / m and f	.*tn* you, your
.*f* he, his, its, him, it .*s* she, her, its, it	3rd person m f / m and f	.*sn* they, their, them

Uses of the suffix-pronouns

Suffix-pronouns have three main uses:

  (i) They are used to denote the person *performing an action*

  e.g. ⌇ *dd.s* (verb *dd* +suffix 3rd person fem *s*) 'she says'

  ⌇ *sdm.i* (verb *sdm* +suffix 1st person sing) 'I say'.

  (ii) They are used to show *possession*

  e.g. ⌇ (noun *pr* +suffix 2nd person m) 'your house'

  ⌇ (noun *snt* +suffix 3rd person m) 'his sister'.

 (iii) They are used *after prepositions*

  e.g. ⌇ *n.i* 'to me'

  ⌇ *hn'.sn* 'with them'.

2. *Dependent pronouns*, which are not as closely attached to a preceding word as the suffix-pronouns, can never stand as the first word of a sentence.

The dependent pronouns are written as follows:

Singular		Plural
wi I, me	1st person m and f	*n* we, us
tw thou, thee / *tn* thou, thee	2nd person m / f m and f	*tn* you
sw he, him, it / *sy* she, her, it / *st* it	3rd person m / f / n m and f	*sn* they, them

Uses of the dependent pronouns

The three main uses of the dependent pronouns are:

(i) To denote the object of an action

e.g. 𓏇𓄿𓃀𓎡 𓅱𓀀 *ḥȝb.k wỉ* (verb *ḥȝb* + suffix 2nd person singular + dependent pronoun *wỉ* as object of verb) 'you send me';

𓏙𓅓𓊪𓊪 *rdỉ.f st* (verb *rdỉ* + suffix 3rd person singular + dependent pronoun *st* as object of verb) 'he gives it'.

(ii) After certain particles such as 𓇋𓋴𓏏 *ỉst* 'lo'; � *mk* 'behold'

e.g. 𓄡𓅱𓀀𓅓𓁧𓎡 *mk wỉ m-bȝḥ.k* 'Behold I am before you' (lit: Behold me before you).

(iii) Reflexively

e.g. 𓏙𓀁𓅱𓀀𓁷𓄡𓏏𓀀 *rdỉ.ỉ wỉ ḥr ẖt.ỉ* 'I place myself on my belly'.

Vocabulary to Lesson 7

𓏞𓏛 *sš* scribe

𓋴𓃀𓈖𓇳 *wbn* to rise (of sun)

𓂋𓈙𓅱 *ršw* to rejoice

𓇋𓏠𓈖 *ỉmn* Amun, god

𓅓𓄡𓏏 *m-ḥȝt* in front of

𓋀 *ỉmnt* the West

𓇼𓏏𓉻 var. 𓇼𓏏𓉻 *dwȝt* the Underworld

𓊃𓉻 var. 𓊪 *sbȝ* door

𓈋 var. 𓈋 *ḏw* mountain

𓊝𓏏𓏫 *ȝwt* oblations, gifts

EXERCISE 7

(a) *Write in hieroglyphs and transliteration*

1. This thy beautiful house.
2. His beautiful wife.
3. In his house.
4. Their city.

(b) *Translate into English*

1.

2.

3.

4.

LESSON 8

More biliteral signs

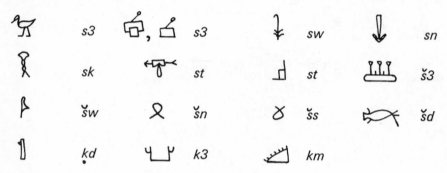

More triliteral signs

Verbs

A verb is a word which tells us what somebody or something does. For example, in the passage 'The frog dived into the water and brought up the ball. With a joyful cry, the princess picked up the ball' : the words 'dived', 'brought up' and 'picked up' are verbs. Schoolchildren are often taught that a verb is a doing word !

In English, the *tense* of a verb refers to the time in which an action takes place. There are three tenses—present, past and future, all, in English, clearly distinct from each other. For example, with the verb 'to arrive', the *present tense* is 'I arrive', the *past tense* is 'I arrived', the *future tense* is 'I shall arrive'.

In Egyptian, the distinctions between tenses are not so clearly marked. Take, for example, the sentence 𓅱𓃀𓈖𓇳 𓂋𓅓𓊪𓏏𓇯 *wbn r' m pt*. 𓅱𓃀𓈖𓇳 (*wbn*) is the verb 'to rise'; 𓂋𓇳 (*r'*) and 𓊪𓏏𓇯 (*pt*) are nouns meaning 'sun' and 'sky' respectively; 𓅓 (*m*) is the preposition 'in'. The sentence can be translated in the following ways:

'the sun rises in the sky' (verb in present tense)

'the sun rose in the sky' (verb in past tense)

'the sun will rise in the sky' (verb in future tense).

Only context will indicate the tense in which to put the verb in translation. Note, here, that in Egyptian the verb is placed at the beginning of the sentence (see further page 101).

Egyptian does have several verb-forms which can be used to clearly indicate past, future, continuous activity, tenses etc. Beginners, however, need not concern themselves with these verb-forms. Instead, we will concentrate on what may be called an 'all-purpose' tense, the *sḏm.f* (pronounced 'sedjemef') form of the verb.

The *sḏm.f* form of the verb

If we analyse the sentence discussed above, *wbn r' m pt,* we find that the subject of the sentence, that is, the noun performing the action of the verb, is *r'* (sun). The verb is *wbn* (rise). In this instance, the *subject* of the sentence (*r'*) has been added on to the *stem of the verb* (*wbn*). This is how the Egyptians made up the *sḏm.f* form of the verb: they took the stem of a verb and added on to it the subject, which could be a noun or a suffix-pronoun.

When describing the various parts of the Egyptian verb, it is usual to take the stem of the verb 𓄔𓄿 *sḏm* 'to hear' as the model. If we add to it as subject the 3rd person masculine singular suffix-pronoun, *f*, the name of the verb form *sḏm.f* is obtained.

The paradigm, or model, of the *sḏm.f* form is as follows:

1st sing. m and f   𓄔𓄿𓀁   *sḏm.i*   I hear

2nd sing. m   𓄔𓄿𓎡   *sḏm.k*   thou hearest

2nd sing. f		*sḏm.t*	thou hearest
3rd sing. m		*sḏm.f*	he (or it) hears
3rd sing. f		*sḏm.s*	she (or it) hears
1st plural m and f		*sḏm.n*	we hear
2nd plural m and f		*sḏm.tn*	you hear
3rd plural m and f		*sḏm.sn*	they hear

When the *subject* of the sḏm.f form is a *suffix-pronoun*, it must *never* be separated from the verb-stem. When, on the other hand, the subject is a *noun*, this can sometimes be separated from the verb-stem:

e.g. *ḏd.s n.f* 'she says to him' *but*

ḏd n.f sš 'the scribe says to him'.

Uses of the sḏm.f form

1. The *sḏm.f* form can be used to express the *present tense* of a verb:
   e.g. *wbn rꜥ m pt* 'the sun rises in the sky'.
2. It can be used to express the *past tense*:
   e.g. *h3b.k sš r nỉwt* 'you sent the scribe into the town'.
3. It can be used to express the *future tense*:
   e.g. *rš s3t.ỉ* 'my daughter shall rejoice'.
4. It can be used to express a *wish* or a *command*:
   e.g. *h3b.k sš* 'may you send the scribe' *or* 'send a scribe!'

The context in which the sentence containing the verb is found will determine the tense of the *sḏm.f* form.

A note on transliteration

Some verbs end in the semi-vowels 𓇋 *i* or 𓅱 *w*, even though these letters may not actually be written out in hieroglyphs e.g. 𓉔𓄿𓂽 *h3i*; 𓆓𓄿𓂽 *ḏ3i*. When the *sḏm.f* form of many of these verbs is *transliterated*, the *i* or the *w* falls away. Thus 𓉐𓂻 *pri* becomes *pr.f* not *pri.f*; 𓂋𓈙𓅱 *ršw* becomes *rš.f* not *ršw.f*. All the verbs ending in *i* or *w* used in this Grammar display this tendency with the exception of 𓂋� *rdi*, which is transliterated *rdi.f*.

Vocabulary to Lesson 8

𓊪 *r* utterance

𓊪𓊪 𓂻 *dpt* boat

𓉔𓄿𓂽 *h3i* to go down

𓅱𓄿𓄿 𓂻 *wi3* sacred barque

𓊮𓂻 *hdi* to fare downstream

𓊮𓏭 *h'i* to appear, to shine

𓈌 *3ht* horizon

𓆓𓏏 *ḏt* eternity

𓆓𓄿𓂻 *ḏ3i* to cross

𓌳𓄿𓄿 *m33* to see

𓅠𓄿 *gmi* to find

�465𓀃 *hkr* hungry man

𓏇 *ini* to bring, to remove

𓈙𓃀𓏇 *šbw* food

EXERCISE 8

(a) *Write in hieroglyphs and transliteration*

  1. Tell your name to the scribe.

  2. You shall say to your son.

3. He rejoices because of her utterances.

4. The scribe sent this boat.

5. He shall fare downstream to the city, his daughter with him.

(b) *Translate into English*

1.

2.

3.

4.

LESSON 9

More biliteral signs

![gm]	*gm*		*t3*		*t3*		* tỉ*
	tp		*tp*		*tm*		*t̠3*
	dỉ		*d̠3*		*dw*		*d̠r*
	d̠d						

More triliteral signs

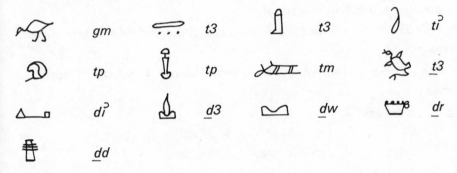

	d̠b3		*d̠bʾ*		*d̠sr*

Sentences and clauses

Word order in sentences

The normal word order in Egyptian sentences is:

1. verb 2. subject (noun or suffix-pronoun) 3. object (noun) 4. adverb or adverbial phrase (preposition +noun):

e.g.

    1. *m3*   2. *s*   3. *sš*   4. *m nỉwt*

    1. saw   2. man   3. scribe   4. in city

    (i.e. the man saw the scribe in the city);

or

1.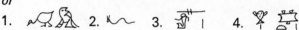

1. *gm*   2. *.f*   3. *s*   4. *ḥr w3t*

1. found   w. he   3. man   4. on road

(i.e. he found the man on the road).

Sometimes, the *normal word order is upset*:

(i) when the *object* is not a noun but a *dependent pronoun* and the *subject* is a noun, then the order is:

   1. verb   2. object (pronoun)   3. subject (noun)   4. adverb or **adverbial** phrase:

   e.g. 1.   2.   3.   4.

   1. *gm*   2. *sw*   3. *s*   4. *ḥr w3t*

   1. found   2. him   3. man   4. on road

   (i.e. the man found him on the road);

(ii) when the *dative* * * is used, then the word order is:

   1. verb   2. subject   3. object   4. dative   5. adverb or adverbial phrase:

   e.g. 1.   2.   3.   4.   5.

   1. *dỉ*   2. *s*   3. *t3*   4. *n ḥkrw*   5. *m nỉwt.f*

   1. gives   2. man   3. bread   4. to hungry   5. in his city

   (i.e. the man gives bread to the hungry in his city);

(iii) when the dative is used, not with a noun but with a *pronoun*, the rule is that *a noun must not precede a pronoun*; and that *the dependent pronoun must not precede a suffix-pronoun*:

   e.g.

   h3b   n.k   sš   s

   sends   to you   scribe   man

   (i.e. the scribe sends the man to you);

   ỉn   n.k   st sš

   brings   to you   it   scribe

   (i.e. the scribe brings it to you).

**In Egyptian, the dative is formed by placing the preposition ~~~~ *n* (see page 84) before a noun or a suffix-pronoun. In the sentences 'I gave money to the man' and 'I gave the money to him' the phrases underlined are datives.

Clauses

If two sentences such as 'the girl was intelligent' and 'the girl was good' are joined together by the conjunction 'and', they are called *clauses*. As each clause in itself makes complete sense, they are said to be *independent* of each other.

Clauses that are connected by conjunctions such as 'after', 'when', 'if', 'though', 'for' are not always independent. For example, in the sentence 'the man was paid after the work had been done', the clause 'the man was paid' can by itself make complete sense, and is therefore an *independent clause*. The clause 'after the work had been done', however, does not make complete sense on its own; it depends upon the first clause in order to make sense. It is called, therefore, a *dependent clause*.

In Egyptian, conjunctions are hardly ever used to indicate dependent clauses. The translator is left to decide for himself the logical connection between clauses. Thus the sentence 𓅨𓏭𓇳𓅱𓃹𓊪𓏏 *wbn r' m pt* which was translated in previous Lessons as an independent clause meaning 'the sun rises in the sky' can also be translated as a dependent clause meaning:

> when the sun rises in the sky
> if the sun rises in the sky
> so that the sun might rise in the sky
> after the sun had risen in the sky etc.,

according to context.

Vocabulary to Lesson 9

rḫ to know

ḏd to tell *n* to someone

ỉb heart, wish (noun)

ỉbỉ to be thirsty

ỉbt thirst

š't despatch

'3 donkey

dšrt the Red Land i.e. the desert

dšrt the Red Crown (of Lower Egypt)

s3 back

ỉrỉ to do, to act, to make

ḥ3t front

ḥ3ty-' local prince

prỉ to go out

ḫrw voice, cry

wṯs to wear, to lift up, to carry

ḥḏt the White Crown (of Upper Egypt)

EXERCISE 9

(a) *Write in hieroglyphs and transliteration*

1. The scribe knows a plan on this day.
2. Your lord has sent to us every good thing.
3. The woman found him upon the road.
4. She gave him bread and beer.
5. He told us his wish.

(b) *Translate into English*

1.

2.

3.

LESSON 10

Negation of the verb form sḏm.f

If an Egyptian wanted to say 'I do *not* hear' instead of 'I hear', he used what is called a *negative word*. The Egyptian language has many negative words; here we shall learn about two of them: ⌇ *n* and ⌇ *nn*, which can be used with the *sḏm.f* form of the verb.

The negative word is placed *before* the verb at the beginning of the sentence, and it changes the meaning of the verb in a rather strange way.

The *sḏm.f* form of the verb, as we have seen, can be used to indicate past, present and future tense. When it is used with the negative words ⌇ or ⌇ this is no longer the case:

1. ⌇ 𓄿𓏛 *n sḏm.f* has *past* meaning:

   e.g. ⌇ 𓄿𓏛

   n ir.i ḫt n ḥȝty-' 'I did not do anything for the prince'.

2. ⌇ 𓄿𓏛 *nn sḏm.f* has *future* meaning:

   e.g. 𓄿𓏛

   nn wṯs.f dšrt 'he shall not wear the Red Crown' *or* 'he shall never wear the Red Crown'.

In order to express the negative of the *present* tense, the element ⌇ *n* is placed *between* the verb-stem and the suffix-pronoun, where this pronoun is used; or *immediately after* the verb-stem when the suffix-pronoun is not used. The negative word ⌇ is then placed before the verb:

e.g. ⌇ 𓄿𓏛

   n pr.n.f 'he does not go out';

   ⌇ 𓄿𓏛

H

n sdm.n.i̯ ḥrw.f 'I do not hear his voice';

n sdm.n nṯr ḥrw.f 'the god does not hear his voice.'

Sentences without verbs

There is no verb 'to be' in Egyptian. If an Egyptian wished to say 'the sun is in the sky', he would simply write   *r' m pt*, which translates as 'sun in sky'; we have to supply both the definite articles and 'is'.

The word order in sentences without verbs is the same as that in sentences with verbs; but since there is no object either in this kind of sentence, the order is:

1. subject   2. adverb or adverbial phrase.

e.g. 1.   2.

1. *s*   2. *m nĩwt*

1. man   2. in town

(i.e. the man is in the town);

or

1.   2.

1. *dpt*   2. *ḥr mw*

1. boat   2. on water

(i.e. the boat is on the water);

or

1.   2.

ḥmt   2. *'3*

1. servant   2. here

(i.e. the servant is here).

m of predication

The Egyptians could not say 'the man is a scribe' but only 'the man is (as) a scribe'. The 'as' is expressed by the preposition   *m*, which means 'in the position of', 'as'. Every sentence is made up of two parts: what is being spoken about (the subject) and what is being said about the subject (the predicate). Hence the term *m* of *predication*: the words introduced by this *m* describe the subject of the sentence.

e.g. *s m sš* 'the man is a scribe'

ḥmt m ḥmt 'the woman is a servant'

Vocabulary to Lesson 10

mhy to be neglectful, to be forgetful, *ḥr* about

bỉnt evil

ḏwỉ evilly

nfrt good

ḳ3 to raise

r-pr temple

rmṯ people

ʿḳ to enter

wstn to stride

dw3 to adore

sns to worship

sns to worship

wḏḥw altar

ỉʿḥ moon

ʿ3 here (adverb)

EXERCISE 10

(a) *Write in hieroglyphs and transliteration*

1. I shall not be neglectful with regard to any counsel of my lord.
2. He does not speak (either) good (or) evil.
3. The man is in this city.
4. His daughter is in the house.
5. Behold, thou art my servant.

(b) *Translate into English*

1.

2.

3.

4.

5.

LESSON 11

Peculiarities of hieroglyphic writing

The reader will find in the Vocabularies a number of spellings which do not seem to conform to the rules of hieroglyphic writing so far learned. The following paragraphs will deal with six kinds of 'peculiar' writing.

Abbreviations

Abbreviated writings are commonly used in monumental inscriptions, stereotyped phrases, titles, etc.

e.g.

nsw king

nsw-biͣt King of Upper and Lower Egypt (lit: he who belongs to the reed of Upper Egypt and the bee of Lower Egypt)

nṯr nfr the good god (epithet of king)

k3 nḫt strong bull (epithet of king)

wḥm 'nḫ repeating life (epithet of dead person)

m3' ḫrw justified (lit: true of voice, epithet applied to dead person, equivalent to our 'deceased')

ḏd mdw for recitation, to be recited

𓋹𓊃𓋴 *'nḫ wḏ3 snb* 'may he live, be prosperous, be healthy' (formula recited as mark of respect when king is mentioned)

𓄂 *ḥ3ty-'* local prince (lit: foremost in position)

𓊃 , 𓊃 *sp sn* twice, used:

(a) to indicate that a sign or signs are repeated e.g. 𓀁𓋴𓏭 *sksk* 'to destroy'

(b) to indicate repetition of a word to convey superlative—like 'very', 'much'

𓅓𓂋𓉐 *ỉmy-r pr* steward (lit: overseer of the house)

Sportive writings

𓄻 *ỉmy-r* overseer (for 𓅓𓂋 *ỉmy-r*); the hieroglyph 𓄻 depicts a tongue, i.e. 'what is in the mouth'; hence the meaning 'overseer' is a pun.

Abbreviated writings

A few words almost never spell out the complete word:

𓂋𓏤𓏥 *rmṯ* men, people

𓋬 *ḥnkt* beer

Composite signs and monograms

1. Sometimes the ideogram is combined with a phonogram:

𓇋𓇋 *ỉỉ* come

𓇋𓊔 *ỉs* go

 *ms* bring

 *šm* go

 *sšm* lead

 *ỉn* bring

2. Some common monograms:

 *tr* season

 *rnp* be young

 *rs*(*w*) south

 *šm'w* Upper Egypt

 *ẖrt-hrw* daytime

 *ẖr*(*t*)-*nṯr* necropolis

 *'ḥ* palace

 *wḏ'* divide

Graphic transposition

Sometimes signs are transposed, usually to give a more pleasing appearance:

 for  *tw*

⟨glyph⟩ for ⟨glyph⟩ *t3*

⟨glyph⟩ for ⟨glyph⟩ *wd*

⟨glyph⟩ for ⟨glyph⟩ *wd3*

⟨glyph⟩ for   *mr* 'pyramid'; this word is never written ⟨glyph⟩

Honorific transpositions

With certain words, such as 'king' (⟨glyph⟩ *nsw*), 'god' (⟨glyph⟩ *ntr*), there is a tendency to write the word *before* closely connected words which are, in speech, pronounced first. This convention is observed in order to honour an important personnage. Abbreviated writings are frequent in such cases:

⟨glyph⟩   *hm-ntr* servant of god (priest)

⟨glyph⟩   *dw3-ntr* praise, thank

⟨glyph⟩   *hwt-ntr* temple (lit: mansion of god)

⟨glyph⟩   *sntr* incense

⟨glyph⟩   *s3 nsw* prince (lit: son of the king)

⟨glyph⟩   *pr nsw* palace (lit: house of the king)

⟨glyph⟩   *htp di nsw* an offering which the king gives

⟨glyph⟩   *mi R'* like Re

⟨glyph⟩   *mry imn* beloved of Amun

⟨glyph⟩   *nsw* king, originally *ni-swt* 'he who belongs to the reed'.

Hints on reading hieroglyphs

At all times, when reading hieroglyphs, it is as well to remember that the 'rules' were often broken. Lack of space sometimes forced a scribe to abbreviate his inscriptions by using fewer signs. Determinatives were often left out; plural signs and feminine endings were omitted. As we have seen above, spellings could vary.

At this stage, it is not necessary for the beginner to know why spellings varied. If he learns the hieroglyphic groups and their transliterations mechanically then he will not need to bother with theories about their etymology.

Vocabulary to Lesson 11

ỉrt 'performing' from verb *ỉrỉ* 'to do'

ḥtp var. to be pleased, satisfied; to rest *ḥr* upon; to set (of sun)

ḥtpw gifts, offerings

dỉ var. of *rdỉ* to give

var. of *nsw* king

3pd var. of goose, bird

rnpt growing thing, vegetable from *rnpỉ* to be young

k3 var. of ox, bull

mr.f 'beloved of him' from var. *mrỉ* to love

m3' ḥrw justified var. of *m3' ḥrw* true of voice

var. *šm'w* Upper Egypt

šm'wt Upper Egyptian

ỉtrt row of shrines

sntr incense

šs alabaster

ḥsb to reckon

t3 mḥw Lower Egypt

ḥnkt offerings

mrḥt unguent

mnḥt clothing

ỉt corn

EXERCISE 11

(a) Reading exercise 1

Study the following passage which is typical of inscriptions on Egyptian funerary stelae. The presentation of funerary offerings was called *ỉrt ḥtp-dỉ-nsw* 'performing (the rite called) "a boon-which-the-king-gives"'. From early on in Egyptian history, the phrase *ḥtp-dỉ-nsw* was used in reference to favours, such as gifts of clothing, food and drink, bestowed by a king upon his subjects. It seems that eventually all funerary gifts were considered to be gifts of the king to deities such as Osiris, the king of the dead, Anubis, the god of embalmment, or Geb, the earth-god ; and that these deities passed on the gifts to the dead owner of the tomb in which the inscription is found.

e.g. Funerary wishes from the tomb of the Theban noble, Amenemhet (Dynasty XVIII) :

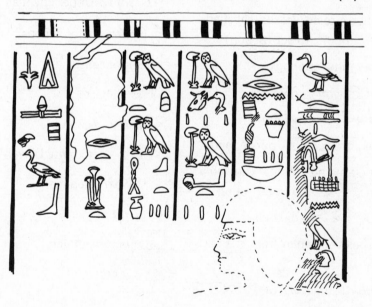

Transcription, transliteration and translation:

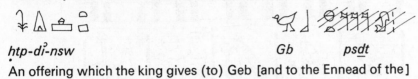

ḥtp-di-nsw   Gb   *psḏt*

An offering which the king gives (to) Geb [and to the Ennead of the]

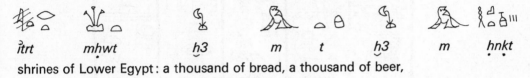

ỉtrt   *mḥwt*   *ḫ3*   *m*   *t*   *ḫ3*   *m*   *ḥnkt*

shrines of Lower Egypt: a thousand of bread, a thousand of beer,

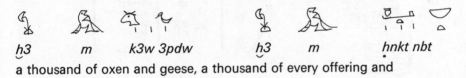

ḫ3   *m*   *k3w 3pdw*   *ḫ3*   *m*   *ḥnkt nbt*

a thousand of oxen and geese, a thousand of every offering and

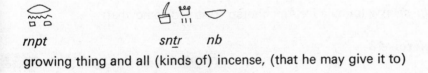

rnpt   *snṯr*   *nb*

growing thing and all (kinds of) incense, (that he may give it to)

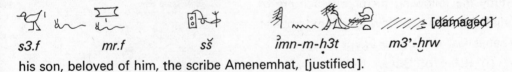

s3.f   *mr.f*   *sš*   *ỉmn-m-ḥ3t*   *m3'-ḫrw*

his son, beloved of him, the scribe Amenemhat, [justified].

(b) Reading exercise 2

Transcribe, transliterate and translate the following *ḥtp-di-nsw* formula from the tomb of Amenemhet. Note that in this formula, the recipient is the son of Amenemhet, a scribe named Amenhotep:

htp-di-nsw formula for Amenhotep (restored somewhat)

(c) Reading exercise 3

Study the following pictures which are of reliefs found in two New Kingdom tombs at Thebes (Luxor), Upper Egypt.

(i) Relief of Queen Nefertari, wife of Ramesses II of Dynasty XIX: transliterate and translate the hieroglyphs on the right-hand side of the picture:

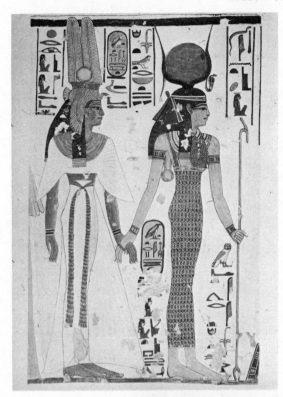

(ii) *Left*:
Relief from the tomb of Nefertari: transliterate and translate the hieroglyphs at the top of the relief:

(iii) *Below*:
Relief from the tomb of King Horemheb, Dynasty XVIII: transliterate and translate the hieroglyphs in the picture (remember to read into the faces of animals etc.):

KEY TO EXERCISE 1

(3) [hieroglyphs] ; [hieroglyphs] ; [hieroglyphs] ; [hieroglyphs] ;

[hieroglyphs] ; [hieroglyphs] ; [hieroglyphs] ; [hieroglyphs]

KEY TO EXERCISE 2

(2) [hieroglyphs] ; [hieroglyphs] ; [hieroglyphs] ; [hieroglyphs] ;

[hieroglyphs] ; [hieroglyphs] ; [hieroglyphs] ; [hieroglyphs] ;

[hieroglyphs] ; [hieroglyphs] ; [hieroglyphs] ; [hieroglyphs] ;

[hieroglyphs] ; [hieroglyphs] ; [hieroglyphs]

KEY TO EXERCISE 3

(a) 1. [hieroglyphs]
'wy

2. [hieroglyphs]
mnty

3. [hieroglyphs]
spty

4. [hieroglyphs]
rnpt 20

5. [hieroglyphs]
ḥf3w 75

6. [hieroglyphs]
dmỉ ẖ3

(b) 1. 2 sides (*w3t 2*)

  2. 365 gods (*365 n ntrw*)

  3. 35 years (*rnpt 35*)

  4. ten thousand men (*s 10,000*)

  5. one hundred jugs of beer (*ḥnkt ds 100*)

KEY TO EXERCISE 4

(a) 1.   *pr pn nfr*

  2.   *nfrt tn*

  3.   *ḥmt nt ḥm ntr*

  4.   *pr nb*

  5.   *imy-r mnḫ n niwt*

(b) 1. an efficient overseer of fowlers (*imy-r sḫty mnḫ*)

  2. all good produce of the country (*inw nb(w) nfr(w) n sḫt*)

  3. every good thing (*ḫt nbt nfrt*)

  4. water for the father of the man (*mw n it s*)

  5. the handmaidens of the mistress of the house (*b3kwt nt ḥnwt nt pr*)

KEY TO EXERCISE 5

(a) 1.   *r ky bw*

  2.   *n Gb ḥn' R'*

  3.   *m rn pn wr*

  4.   *m t3w nbw*

  5.   *m-b3h Ptḥ*

(b) 1. night and day (*grḥ mỉ hrw*)

2. to the limits of the four supports of heaven (*r drw sḫnwt nt pt*)

3. in the sanctuary of Ptah (*m ỉwnn n Ptḥ*)

4. on this beautiful day (*m hrw pn nfr*)

KEY TO EXERCISE 6

1. *sḥtp-ỉb-R'*   *ỉmn-m-ḥ3t*

   (the heart of Re is satisfied)   (Amun is at the beginning)

   Sehetep-ib-Re   Ammenemes I (Dynasty XII)

2. *ḫpr-k3-R'*   *s-n-Wsrt**

   (the spirit of Re comes into being)   (man of (the goddess) Wosret)

   Kheper-ka-Re   Sesostris I (Dynasty XII)

                                           *this was formerly read *wsrtsn*
                                              (Usertsen), the version found in many
                                              of the early books on Egypt

3. *ḫ'-k3w-R'*   *s-n-Wsrt*

   (the spirits of Re appear)

   Kha-kau-Re   Sesostris III (Dynasty XII)

4. *n-m3't-R'*   *ỉmn-m-ḥ3t*

   (belonging to the Truth of Re)

   Ne-maat-Re   Amenemmes III (Dynasty XII)

5. *m3't-k3-R'*   *ḥ3t-špswt*

   (Truth is the spirit of Re)   (foremost of noble women)

   Maat-ka-Re   Hatshepsut (Queen) (Dynasty XVIII)

6. *mn-ḫpr-R'*   *Ḏḥwty-ms*
    (the form of Re remains)   (born of Thoth)
    Men-heper-Re   Tuthmosis III (Dynasty XVIII)

7. *nb-m3't-R'*   *ỉmn-ḥtp—ḥk3 w3st*
    (lord of the Truth of Re)   (Amun is satisfied—ruler of Thebes)
    Neb-maat-Re   Amenophis III (Dynasty XVIII)

8. *nb-ḫprw-R'*   *twt-'nh-ỉmn*
    (lord of the forms of Re)   (living image of Amun)
    Neb-heperu-Re   Tutankhamun (Dynasty XVIII)

9. *mn-m3't-R'*   *sṯ-y—mr-n-Ptḥ*
    (the Truth of Re remains)   (Seti beloved of Ptah)
    Men-maat-Re   Sethos I (Dynasty XIX)

10. *wsr-m3't-R'-stp-n-R'*   *R'-msw—mry-ỉmn*
    (powerful Truth of Re, chosen of Re) (born of Re—beloved of Amun)
    User-maat-Re-setep-en-Re   Ramesses II (Dynasty XIX)

KEY TO EXERCISE 7

(a) 1.   *pr.k pn nfr*

2.   *ḥmt.f nfrt*

3.   *m pr.f*

4.   *nỉwt.sn*

(b) 1. his little daughter (*s3t . f šrit*)

  2. my wife, together with my daughter (*ḥmt . i ḥn' s3t . i*)

  3. Lo, I am before you (*ist wi ḫft ḥr . k*)

  4. Behold you are with me as my servant (*mk tw ḥn' . i m b3k . i*)

KEY TO EXERCISE 8

(a) 1.   *dd . k rn . k n sš*

  2.   *dd . k n s3 . k*

  3.   *rš . f ḥr r . s*

  4.   *h3b sš dpt tn*

  5.   *ḥd . f r niwt s3t . f ḥn' . f*

(b) 1. Re crosses the sky in his barque (*d3 R' pt m wi3 . f*)

  2. The man goes down to the city upon another road (*h3 s r niwt ḥr kt w3t*)

  3. The father sent his son to the city (*h3b it s3 . f r niwt*)

  4. The sun appears upon the horizon and shines in the sky (*ḫ' r' m 3ḫt wbn . f m pt*)

KEY TO EXERCISE 9

(a) 1.   *rḫ sš sḫr m hrw pn*

  2.   *h3b n . n nb . tn ḫt*

              nbt nfrt

3. gm.n sw ḥmt ḥr w3t

4. rdỉ.s n.f t ḥnḳt

5. ḏd.f n.n ỉb.f

(b) 1. I gave bread to the hungry and beer to the thirsty (rdỉ.ỉt n ḥḳrw ḥnḳt n ỉbw)

2. Our good lord sends us a despatch about it (h3b n.n nb.n nfr š't ḥr.s)

3. After the servant had brought the donkey, he placed himself on its back (ỉn ḥm '3 dỉ.f sw ḥr s3.f)

KEY TO EXERCISE 10

(a) 1. nn mhy ḥr sḥr nb n nb.ỉ

2. n ḏd.n.f nfrt bỉnt

3. s m nỉwt tn

4. s3t.f m pr

5. mk tw m b3k.ỉ

(b) 1. I did not raise my voice in the temple of my god (n k3 ḥrw.ỉ m r-pr n nṯr.ỉ)

2. I do not do anything against any people evilly (n ỉr.n.ỉ ḫt nbt dwỉ r rmt nb)

3. He shall not receive bread (from) upon the altar of any god (nn šsp.f t ḥr wdḥw n(y) nṯr nb

4. The moon rejoices when the sun is in his horizon (ršỉ 'ḥ r' m 3ḫt.f)

5. This beautiful woman is my sister; she does not speak any evil (nfrt tn m snt.ỉ n ḏd.n.s ḏwt nbt)

KEY TO EXERCISE 11

(c)   *Reading exercise 3*

    (i)   *Transliteration:* m3' ḥrw ḥr wsỉr nṯr '3 nb ỉmntt

         Translation: Justified before Osiris, the great god, lord of the West.

    (ii) *Transliteration:* ḏd mdw ỉn 3st

         Translation: For recitation by Isis.

                                  ḥmt-nsw wrt nbt t3wy

                                  The great royal wife (i.e. queen) mistress of the Two Lands

                                  (nfrt-ỉry mrt n(t) mwt)

                                  (Nefertari beloved of Mut)

                                  m3' ḥrw ḥr wsỉr nṯr '3

                                  justified before Osiris, the great god.

    (iii) *Transliteration:* ḏd mdw ỉn 3st wrt

         Translation: For recitation by Isis the great,

                                  ḥnwt t3wy

                                  mistress of the Two Lands.

                                  wsỉr nsw (ḏsr ḫprw r' stp n r')

                                  The Osiris, King (sacred form of Re, chosen of Re)

                                  s3 r' (ḥr m ḥb mry n ỉmn)

                                  the Son of Re (Horemheb beloved of Amun)

                                  m3' ḥrw ḥr (wsỉr)

                                  justified before (Osiris).

Notes

Osiris is the god of the dead who resides in the Underworld. 'The West' is a term used for the Underworld. Isis is the wife of Osiris. Mut is the wife of the god, Amun, of Thebes. Re is the sun god. Every dead person becomes 'an Osiris'; therefore, the reference to 'the Osiris' in example (iii) means that the king mentioned therein is dead.

LIST OF HIEROGLYPHIC SIGNS

The following list contains most of the hieroglyphic signs used in this book, divided into groups. Within the groups, each sign is listed together with the name of the object it depicts, its uses and its transliteration/s (where applicable—some signs have no sound value but are found as determinatives (see further p. 66ff.) or ideographs only).

Sign	Depicts	Meaning etc.
Male figures		
	seated man	ideograph ; determinative
	seated man and woman with plural strokes	det.
	man with hand to mouth	det.
	child seated with hand to mouth	det.
	bent man leaning on stick	ideo. ; det.
	upright man with stick	ideo. ; det.
	man with both arms raised	det.
	man striking with stick	det.
	seated god	det. ; ideo.
	seated king	det. ; ideo.
	noble seated on chair	det.
	mummy case	det.
	god with head of falcon with sun's disk on head	ideo. or det. for sun god e.g. Re
	god with head of ibis	ideo. or det. for god Thoth

Sign	Depicts	Meaning etc.
Male figures		
	god with head of pig (?)	ideo. for god Seth
	god with arms upraised	ideo. for god Ḥeḥ hence phon-etically *ḥḥ*
Female figures		
	seated woman	det.
	goddess with feather on head	ideo. or det. for Maat, goddess of truth
Parts of the human body		
	head in profile	ideo.; det.
	face	ideo.; phon. *ḥr*
	eye	ideo.; phon. *ỉr*
	nose, eye and cheek	ideo.; det.
	mouth	ideo.; phon. r
	upper lip with teeth	ideo.
	arms outstretched	ideo.; phon. *k3*
	arms holding shield and axe	ideo.
	arms outstretched	ideo.; phon. *n*
	forearm	ideo.; phon. '
	arm and hand holding loaf	det.; phon. *mỉ*; *m*; *d*
	hand	ideo.; det.; phon. *d*
	finger	ideo.; det.; phon. *ḏb'*

Sign	*Depicts*	*Meaning etc.*
	phallus	det.; phon. *mt*; *ḫmt*
	legs walking	ideo.; det.
	legs walking backwards	det.
	leg	ideo.; det.
	foot	phon. *b*
	foot surmounted by vase with water flowing from it	ideo. (purity)

Mammals

	bull	ideo.; det.
	ass	det.
	kid	phon. *ỉb*
	recumbent lion	ideo.; phon. *rw*
	desert hare	phon. *wn*

Invertebrata

	dung-beetle	ideo.; phon. *ḫpr*
	bee	ideo.; phon. *bỉt*

Birds

	Egyptian vulture	ideo.; phon. *3*
	buzzard	phon. *tỉw*
	vulture	phon. *mwt*
	owl	phon. *m*
	crested ibis	ideo.; phon. *3ḫ*
	sacred ibis	det. Thoth

Sign	Depicts	Meaning etc.
Birds		
	black ibis	phon. *gm*
	cormorant	phon. '*ḳ*
	swallow	phon. *wr* (N.B. swallow tail)
	sparrow	det. (N.B. rounded tail)
	goose	det.; phon. *gb*
	duck	det.; phon. *s3*
	duck flying	ideo.; phon. *p3*
	quail chick	phon. *w*

Signs grouped according to shape

Tall narrow signs

Sign	Depicts	Meaning etc.
	bundle of reeds	phon. *ỉs*
	bricklayer's tool?	phon. *ḳd*
	another form of sign above	
	butcher's knife	ideo.; phon. *nm*
	fire-drill	phon. *ḏ3*
	pestle	ideo.; phon. *tỉ*
	walking stick	ideo.; phon. *md*
	club	ideo.; phon. *ḥm*
	dagger	det.
	flowering reed	ideo.; phon. *ỉ*
	feather	ideo.; phon. *šw*

Sign	*Depicts*	*Meaning etc.*
	bare palm-branch	det.; phon. *rnp*
	lotus	ideo.; phon. *ḫ3*
	folded cloth	phon. *s*
	pod	phon. *nḏm*
	feather on stand	ideo. (west)
	mast	phon. *'ḥ'*
	sceptre	ideo.; det.; phon. *w3s*
	sceptre	phon. *ḏ'm*
	sceptre	ideo. (Thebes)
	head and neck of canine	ideo.; phon. *wsr*
	crook	ideo.; det.; phon. *ḫḳ3*
	crook	phon. *'wt*
	throw-stick	det.
	pieces of wood tied together	ideo. (vigilant, etc.); phon. *rs*
	supporting pole	ideo.; det.
	post of balance	det.
	not known	phon. *nḏ*
	cloth on pole	ideo. (divinity); phon. *nṯr*
	mace	ideo.; phon. *ḥḏ*
	cord on stick	phon. *wḏ* or *wd*
	chisel	phon. *mr*
	sceptre	ideo.; det.; phon. *'b3*

Sign	Depicts	Meaning, etc.
Tall narrow signs		
	heart and windpipe	phon. *nfr*
	lung and windpipe	phon. *sm3*
	milk jug in net	det.; phon. *mỉ*
	oar	det.; phon. *ḥrw*
	arrow-head	ideo.; phon. *sn*
	two crossed planks	ideo.; phon. *ỉmỉ*
	loaf	ideo. (give)
	receptacle	det.; phon. *ḥn*
	three foxes' skins	phon. *ms*
	sandal-strap	ideo.; phon. *'nḫ*
	column	ideo.; phon. *ḏd*
	column	ideo.; phon. *ỉwn*
	palace	ideo.
	wick of twisted flax	phon. *ḥ*
	swab	det.; phon. *sk*; *w3ḥ*
	reed-floats	phon. *ḏb3*
	seat	ideo.; phon. *st*
	cow's skin pierced by arrow	det.
	scribe's outfit	ideo.; det.
	water-pot	ideo.; det.; phon. *ḥs*
	clump of papyrus	phon. *ḥ3*

Sign	Depicts	Meaning etc.
	plant	ideo.; phon. *sw*
	two rushes	phon. *nn*
	bowl with legs	phon. *inỉ*
	chisel	det.; ideo.; *mnḫ* 'be efficient'
	lasso	phon. *w3*
	finger	ideo.; det.; phon. *ḏbʿ*
	arms holding shield and axe	ideo.
	sail	ideo.; det.
	papyrus roll	ideo.; phon. *mḏ3t*
	arms extended	ideo.; phon. *k3*
	leg and hoof of ox	ideo.; phon. *wḥm*

Low broad signs

Sign	Depicts	Meaning etc.
	sky	ideo.; det.; phon. *ḥry*
	garden pool	ideo.; phon. *š*
	sandy tract	ideo.; phon. *ỉ*
	flat land with grains of sand	ideo.; det.; phon. *t*
	not known	phon. *m3ʿ*
	not known	phon. *ỉm*
	netting needle filled with twine	ideo.; phon. *ʿd*
	papyrus roll	ideo.; phon. *mḏ3t*
	loaf on reed mat	ideo.; phon. *ḥtp*
	crescent moon	ideo.; det.

Sign	Depicts	Meaning etc.
Low broad signs		
	upper lip with teeth	ideo.
	tongue of ox (?)	ideo.; phon. *ns*
	water skin	phon. *šd*
	sandy hill country	ideo.; det.
	whip	phon. *mḥ*
	whip	phon. *mḥ*
	bolt	ideo.; phon. *s*
	wooden column	phon. *'3*
	harpoon	ideo.
	adze	ideo.; phon. *nw*
	adze on block of wood	ideo.; det.; phon. *stp*
	tethering rope	phon. *t*
	elephant tusk	det.; phon. *bḥ*; *ḥ*
	finger	ideo.; det.; phon. *ḏkr*
	sledge	phon. *tm*
	road with shrubs	ideo.; det.
	door	ideo.; det.; phon. *'3*
	channel with water	ideo.; det.; phon. *mi*ꜣ
	mouth	ideo.; phon. *r*
	basket	ideo.; phon. *nb*
	basket with handle	phon. *k*

Sign	Depicts	Meaning etc.
	alabaster basin	det.; phon. $ḥb$
	reed fence	phon. $šsp$
	oxyrhynchus fish	ideo.; phon. $ẖ3$
	ripple of water	phon. n
	three ripples of water	ideo.; phon. mw
	a fish	det.; phon. $ỉn$
	forepart of lion	ideo.
	goat skin	ideo.; phon. $ẖn(w)$
	draught-board	phon. mn
	animal's belly	ideo.; phon. $ẖ$
	house	ideo.; phon. pr
	backbone	ideo.; phon. $3w$
	sickle	ideo.; phon. $m3$
	forearm with hand holding round loaf	phon. $mỉ$; m
	reeds	ideo.; det.; phon. sm
	horns of ox	ideo.; phon. wp
	hoe	det.; phon. mr
	phallus	det.; phon. mt
	branch	ideo.; det.; phon. $ḫt$
	sky with star hanging beneath	det.
	herb	det.; phon. $ḫn$; $ỉs$

Sign	Depicts	Meaning etc.
Low broad signs		
	bow-string	ideo.; det.; phon. *rwd*
	pool with lotuses	ideo.; phon. *š3*
	sun rising over hill	ideo.
	sandy hill	ideo.; phon. *dw*
	band of string or linen	det.; phon. *'rḳ*
	back of something	ideo.; phon. *s3*
	horned viper	ideo.; phon. *f*
	cobra	phon. *d*
	forearm	ideo.; phon. '
Low narrow signs		
	stool	phon. *p*
	stone slab	det.
	tongue of land	det.
	irrigation canal	det.
	sandy hill-slope	phon. *ḳ*
	loaf	det.
	bread	ideo.; phon. *t*
	hill over which sun is rising	ideo.; phon. *ḫ'*
	back of something	ideo.; phon. *s3*
	piece of crocodile skin	phon. *km*

Sign	Depicts	Meaning etc.
	bowl with smoke of incense rising from it	ideo.; det.
	basket of fruit or grain	det.
	bundle of flax tied at top	det.; phon. dr
	potter's kiln	ideo.; phon. $t3$
	jar-stand	ideo.; det.; phon. g
	butcher's block	phon. hr
	well full of water	det.; phon. hm; $bi3$
	well full of water	det.; phon. hm; $bi3$
	heart	ideo.
	cord	ideo.; phon. $šs$
	loop of cord	phon. $šn$
	hobble for cattle	phon. md
	ear of ox?	ideo.; det.; phon. idn
	sun	ideo.; det.
	moon with lower half obscured	ideo.; det.; phon. psd
	placenta?	phon. h
	threshing floor covered with grain	det.; phon. sp
	village with cross-roads	ideo.; det.
	cartouche in original round form rather than the later	det.

Sign	Depicts	Meaning etc.
Low narrow signs		
(sunshine sign)	sunshine	det. ; ideo. ; phon. *wbn*
(flower sign)	flower ?	phon. *wn*
(coil sign)	coil of rope	det. ; phon. *šn*
(doubtful sign)	doubtful	phon. *gs*
(star sign)	star	ideo. ; det. ; phon. *sb3* ; *dw3*
(bowl sign)	bowl	phon. *nw*
(beer-jug sign)	beer-jug	ideo. ; det.
(frog sign)	frog	det
(tadpole sign)	tadpole	phon. *ḥfn*
(reed shelter sign)	reed shelter	ideo.. ; phon *h*

EGYPTIAN-ENGLISH VOCABULARY

3

3wt gifts

3pd goose, bird

3pd goose, bird

3ḫt horizon

3st Isis

ỉ

ỉʿḥ moon

ỉwnn sanctuary

ỉb heart

ỉbt thirst

ỉbỉ to be thirsty

ỉmy-r overseer

ỉmy-r overseer

ỉmn Amun (god)

ỉmnt the West *ỉmntt*

ỉn by

ỉnỉ to bring

ỉnw produce

ỉrỉ to do, act, make

K

ỉrt eye

ỉt corn

ỉt father

ỉtrt row of shrines

ʿ

ʿ3 donkey

ʿ3 great

ʿ3 here

ʿnḫ to live

ʿḳ to enter

w

w3st Thebes

w3t road, path, way

wỉ3 sacred barque

wbn to rise

wbn to shine

wr great

wr prince, noble

wsỉr Osiris

wsr powerful

Wsrt Wosret (goddess)

wstn to stride

wṯs to wear, carry lift, up

wdḥw altar

b

b3kt handmaiden

bint evil

bw place

p

pr house

pri to go out

psḏt Ennead

pt sky

Ptḥ Ptah (god)

m

m in, from, with

m on, in

m33 to see

m3' ḥrw justified

M3't Maat, goddess of Truth

m3't truth

m3' ḥrw justified

mi like

mw water

mwt Mut

mn to remain

mnḫ to be efficient

mnḫt clothing

mnt thigh

mri to love

mry beloved

mrḥt unguent

mhy to neglect, forget

mḥ cubit

m-ḫ3t in front of

m-ḫt after

ms born

n

n to, of

nb any, every, all

nb lord, master

nfr good, beautiful, happy

nfrt good

nḥḥ eternity

nsw king (of Upper Egypt)

nsw-bit king (of Upper and Lower Egypt)

ntr god

r

r mouth

r to, against

r utterance

R' Re (sun god)

R' Re

R' Re

r' sun

r' sun

r-pr temple

rmt people

rn name

rnpt vegetable

rnpt year

rḫ to know

ršw to rejoice

rdỉ to give, place

r-drw to the limits

h

hȝỉ to go down

hȝb to send

hrw day, daytime

ḥ

ḥȝt front, forehead

ḥȝty-' local prince

ḥfȝw snake

ḥm Majesty

ḥm(t) servant

ḥm-ntr priest

ḥmt woman, wife

ḥn' with

ḥnwt mistress

ḥnwt mistress

ḥnkt offerings

ḥnkt beer

ḥr face, upon

ḥs to freeze

ḥsỉ to turn back

ḥsb to reckon

ḥkȝ ruler

ḥkr hungry man

ḥtpw gifts, offerings

ḥdt White Crown (of Upper Egypt)

ḫ

ḫʿi to appear, shine

ḫʿi to appear

ḫpr to become

ḫprw form

ḫft in front of, before

ḫr before

ḫrw voice, cry

ḫt thing

ḫdi to fare downstream

ẖ

ẖt belly, body

s

s man

s3 back

s3 son

s3t daughter

sb3 door

sbw food

spt lip

sns to worship

snt sister

sntr incense

sḥtp to pacify

sḥtp to satisfy

sḫnt four supports of heaven

sḫr plan, counsel

sḫt country

sḫty fowler, peasant

sš scribe

st woman

sti Seti (king)

stp choice

sḏm to hear, obey

šʿt despatch

špsi to be noble

šmʿw Upper Egypt

šrr small

šs alabaster

šsp to accept, receive

šsp daylight

šsp palm (unit of length)

šsp statue

k

k3 to raise

k

k3 ox, bull

k3 ox, bull

k3 spirit

ky other, another m.

kmt the Black Land (Egypt)

kt another, other f.

g

Gb Geb (god)

gmỉ to find

grḥ night

t

t bread

t3 earth

t3wy the Two Lands (Egypt)

t3 mḥw Lower Egypt

twt image, statue

d

dw3 to adore

dw3t Underworld

dpt boat

dmỉ town

drt hand

ds jug

dšrt Red Crown (of Lower Egypt)

dšrt red land (desert)

d̠

d̠3ỉ to cross

d̠w mountain

d̠wỉ evilly

d̠wt evil, sadness

Dḥwty Thoth (god)

d̠sr sacred

d̠t eternity

d̠d to say, tell *n* to someone

d̠d mdw 'for recitation'

ENGLISH-EGYPTIAN VOCABULARY

A

accept

act

adore

against

alabaster

all

altar

Amun

another

any

appear

B

back

beautiful

beer

before

belly

bird

Black Land (Egypt)

boat

body

born

bread

bring

bull

by

C

carry

choose

city

clothing

corn

counsel

country

cross

cubit

D

daughter

day

daylight

daytime

desert

despatch

do

donkey

door

E

earth

efficient

Egypt

Ennead

enter

eternity

every

evil

evilly

eye

F

face

father

find

food

forget

'for recitation'

freeze

from

front

G

Geb

gifts

give

god

go down

go out

good

goose

great

H

hand

handmaiden

happy

hear

heart

here

horizon

house

hungry man

I

image

in

incense

J

jug

K

king

know

L

lift up

like

lip

live

lord

love

Lower Egypt

M

majesty

make

man

mistress

moon

mountain

mouth

N

name

night

O

obey

of ,

offerings ,

other ,

overseer ,

ox , ,

P

pacify

palm

peasant

people

place

plan

powerful

priest

prince

produce

R

raise

Re

receive

recitation   see 'for recitation'

reckon

Red Crown

rejoice

rise

road

ruler

S

sail downstream

sanctuary

satisfy

say

scribe

see

send

servant

shine

shrines

sister

sky

small

snake

son

statue

stride

sun

supports (four) of heaven

T

tell

temple

Thebes

thigh

thing

thirst

thirsty

this

Thoth

to

town

turn back

Two Lands (Egypt)

U
Underworld
unguent
upon
Upper Egypt
utterance

V
vegetable
voice

W
water
wear
West
White Crown
wife
with
woman
worship

Y
year

FURTHER READING

A. Erman, *'The Ancient Egyptians; a sourcebook of their writings'*, Harper Torchbooks, N.Y., 1966.

R. O. Faulkner, *'A concise dictionary of Middle Egyptian'*, O.U.P., Oxford, 1964.

Sir Alan Gardiner, *'Egyptian grammar'*, 3rd ed., O.U.P., London, 1966.

G. Posener, *'A dictionary of Egyptian civilization'*, Methuen, London, 1962.

GENERAL INDEX